TRAVELS with JERRY

Global Adventures with Jerry Harju

by Jerry Harju

To Stacey Enjoy! Jerry Harju

TRAVELS with JERRY

Global Adventures with Jerry Harju

by Jerry Harju

Edited by Karen Murr
Cover Design by Stacey Willey

Copyright 2013
Jerry Harju

Published by North Harbor Publishing
Marquette, Michigan

Publishing Coordination by
Globe Printing Inc.
Ishpeming, Michigan

Printed by McNaughton & Gunn Inc. Saline, MI

ISBN 978-0-9788898-7-6

October, 2013

INTRODUCTION

Over the years I've written books with stories of my childhood experiences and antics. As an adult my favorite pastime has been travel. Many people have expressed interest in my wanderings, and I thought it was about time to put together a book about some of my travel adventures.

The book doesn't discuss ordinary trips like Green Bay shopping forays, although I love Green Bay, and Karen and I go there frequently. No, these stories are about journeys more off the beaten path. Some of the trips are *WAY* off the beaten path. I hope you enjoy them.

Jerry Harju
North Harbor Publishing
528 E. Arch St.
Marquette, MI 49855
E-mail: jharju@chartermi.net
Website: www.jerryharju.com

DEDICATION

To Karen, my editor and travel companion,
both on this continent and beyond.

ACKNOWLEDGMENTS

I want to thank the following people who have helped me put this book together. First of all, Karen Murr, my traveling companion and editor of this book, has made significant contributions both to the quality of the prose and the content of many of the stories. Stacey Willey of Globe Printing did a fine job laying out the book manuscript and designing the cover. As ever, Steve Schmidt stepped up and produced the bar code. Finally, I want to acknowledge Skip Vorhees who mentored me on traveling to the North Pole and how to get back alive.

TABLE OF CONTENTS

Books in Print by Jerry Harju

NORTHERN REFLECTIONS

NORTHERN D'LIGHTS

NORTHERN PASSAGES

NORTHERN MEMORIES

NORTHERN TALES NO. 5

HERE'S WHAT I THINK

WAY BACK WHEN

OUR WORLD WAS IN BLACK & WHITE

COLD CASH

THE WITCH'S PICNIC (CD SET)

Other Books in Print by North Harbor Publishing

The U.P. Goes to War
by Larry Chabot

Saving Our Sons
by Larry Chabot

Finland Calling
by Carl Pellonpaa

Life With a View
by Deb Pascoe

DRIVING THE BAJA

I n 1971 I was working in Los Angeles. One day I picked up the *Los Angeles Times* and spotted an article that grabbed my attention. The Mexican government had finally decided to pave the road traversing the length of Baja California.

Baja (pronounced ba-ha) California is the 1000-mile-long peninsula running south from the U. S. border parallel to Mexico's west coast. Since the beginning of time the Baja had been largely uninhabited. In 1971 the only towns of any appreciable size were Tijuana and Ensenada on the north end and La Paz close to the southern tip. Short distances of paved road extended south from Ensenada and north from La Paz, but the area in between was over 800 miles of unpaved two-rut road, often made impassable by drifting sand in the summer and mud in the winter. It was one of the most desolate, treacherous stretches on the planet, and only an utter fool would attempt to drive the entire distance. Now the Mexican government was going to pave over that wonderfully awful dirt road, and if I wanted to be the next utter fool to drive it, I had to do it soon.

I arranged to take three weeks vacation from my job and began preparing for the trip. I bought a cheap aluminum shell for the back of my almost-new Chevy pickup. Books written by the few Baja adventurers advised taking important precautions regarding your vehicle. Another spare tire–two were practically mandatory. Two or three replacement air filters to keep the fine road dust out of the carburetor. A sheet of expanded metal grating, spades, and a garden hoe, all for dealing with getting the truck unstuck. I wondered about the hoe but would shortly find out what it was used for. A large piece of felt for filtering impurities out of the local gasoline as you filled the tank. Finally, I had a stout steel plate welded around the underside of the truck's oil pan to protect it against rocks in the road.

My girlfriend, Cam, thought that the Baja expedition sounded exciting and decided to come along. She immediately began amassing canned goods and cooking utensils for the trip. The day before our departure we were in Cam's driveway loading supplies into the truck. Her neighbor, Pearl, came over and peered into the rear of the pickup, checking all of the stuff we were taking along. She asked Cam if her mama knew that she was going down into Mexico with a man who was carrying two cases of cheap wine in the back of his pickup truck.

The next morning we took off, crossing into Mexico at Tijuana and continuing south to Ensenada–good paved road all the way. But 75 miles south of Ensenada the pavement ended at a gas station that declared in both Spanish and English, "LAST GAS STATION." We nervously topped off the gas tank and continued on. Fifty miles down the dirt road the sun was getting low so we decided to call it a day and pulled off the road.

Cam totally vetoed the idea of sleeping on the ground, convinced that tarantulas and scorpions would be crawling into her sleeping bag. So we unloaded a ton of supplies and equipment in order to be able to roll out the sleeping bags in the back of the truck. I gathered up dried sagebrush for a campfire, and for dinner we had Dinty Moore canned stew and bread, washed down with, of course, my cheap wine.

The following morning dawned sunny and clear. I scrambled out of the truck and gazed around. The empty road stretched off in both directions—no cars, no houses, no people. Some official in Mexico's Department of Highways must have had one too many tequilas the day he labeled this road Mexico's "Highway One."

Realizing that I could make this a truly memorable moment, I filled our plastic bucket with water, stripped off my clothes and began giving myself a bath. The shock of the cold water had me screeching.

"What are you doing out there?" Cam called from her sleeping bag in the truck.

"I'm taking a bath in the middle of Highway One!"

"Get your clothes on. Somebody might see you."

Being seen naked out there wouldn't have been a problem.

For the rest of the morning we didn't see a soul. No animals, not even birds. It was eerily quiet, the only sounds being the truck engine and tires crunching on rocks. The sparse vegetation consisted of scraggly sagebrush and boojum trees. The boojum is a very tall cactus-like plant native to Baja California. The soft trunk is flexible, and when the tree grows tall enough the top flops over, forming a giant question mark as if the boojum was asking, "What the $%^^# are you doing here?"

However, we did see signs of civilization. Every so often we'd encounter the rusting hulk of an abandoned car or truck, a sinister testimony to the fact that this was not a trip to be taken lightly. The wheels were always missing, the vehicle owner or a passerby salvaging whatever they could carry off. I prayed that my almost-new Chevy pickup wouldn't be joining that grim collection of iron ghosts.

Late in the afternoon of our first full day on the dirt road we finally encountered mankind. A small adobe house sitting next to the road displayed a crude sign advertising "Comidas, Cerveza, Gas." Meals, beer, and gas–life's essentials in the Baja.

A man, his wife, and three small children came out to greet us, the kids yelling and running circles around our pickup truck. They didn't speak English, so I trotted out my rusty high-school Spanish and said we'd like some dinner, beer, and gas.

I was carrying two 5-gallon cans filled with U. S. gasoline. I emptied the cans into the truck's tank and told the proprietor to fill them from his 55-gallon drum. It took him over a half hour to hand pump ten gallons into my cans.

Our dinner consisted of beans, tortillas, and Tecate beer. Water was in short supply in the Baja, but we always found plenty of beer, which was fortunate since drinking Mexican beer was more healthful than drinking Mexican water.

We hit the road again and didn't see another soul for the rest of the day. Like driving on the moon except for the occasional rusted-out vehicle and empty beer cans. There were absolutely no road signs. Cam had bought a little ball compass that she had attached to the inside of the windshield with a rubber suction cup. The compass became a source of high anxiety because the road twisted and turned, madly spinning the compass from east, west, north to south when it should have been reading south all the while.

To make matters worse, we'd come to a fork in the road, and, of course, there were no signs. I would arbitrarily take the right fork.

Cam lit up a nervous cigarette. "The compass has been reading 'North' for ten minutes now. We took the wrong fork."

"The books say that all roads lead to La Paz. Drivers just make new roads whenever the old one gets washed out."

She lit another cigarette from the butt of the first one.

The books were right. No matter which fork we took, the road always swung south, heading for La Paz.

When we began using the gasoline sold to us by locals I had to place a piece of felt across the truck's gas tank opening to filter the Mexican gas in my five-gallon cans. It took forever. The first time I did it Cam laughed until she saw the tiny metal pieces caught by the felt filter. Mexican gasoline was as bad as Mexican water.

In the days to follow we got stuck. And we got stuck again. Then we got stuck a third time, and a fourth. The Baja sand was like talcum powder, drifting across the road with the slightest breeze. Fortunately I'd come prepared with two spades, expanded metal grating to put under the wheels, and a garden hoe. One time when we got *REALLY REALLY* stuck the hoe saved our bacon. The sand was so deep that the pickup's transmission housing was hung up on the sand. Laying on my back and reaching under the truck with the hoe I dug the sand out from beneath the transmission and got us free.

Cam had her own personal problem: finding a place to potty. The land was mostly flat desert, offering no privacy. I'd stop the truck, and she'd grab a roll of toilet paper and go marching off into the desert. I mean, she'd go *WAY* off into the desert. Finally I'd yell, "Do it already! We haven't seen anybody for hours!"

"Shaddup!" she'd yell back, looking for a large boojum tree.

Halfway down the peninsula was San Ignacio, the first settlement we encountered large enough to be classified as a village. Jesuit missionaries had built a mission there in the late 1700's. They had also planted numerous date palms that swayed gently as we drove down the main street. San

Ignacio was a welcome oasis, but even more welcome was the hand-painted sign that said, "SHOWERS $1." Cam screamed with delight.

We'd been on the road for a week, using only enough of our precious water to make morning coffee, sparingly wash utensils, and occasionally to brush our teeth. Every square inch on our bodies was impacted with sand. I screeched to a halt next to the sign, grabbing for a couple of dollar bills.

Our faces fell when we laid eyes on the "shower." A tin box resembling a roofless Porta Potty stood on a small hill with an open metal tank attached to one side. Below the hill a woman heated water over an open fire. When a paying customer stepped into the shower and stripped down, the woman's young son would grab a pail of hot water and run up the hill, dump the water into the tank, and run back down the hill for a refill. The water was gravity fed through a pipe into the shower. There was no nozzle so the person inside had to assume various contorted positions to get all body parts beneath the stream of water. Soaping and rinsing had to be quick because when the boy decided he'd made enough trips up the hill your shower was over. Cam said, "If you think I'm getting in that thing you're crazy!" She did, though.

And, of course, no trip to Mexico would be complete without a bout of–you guessed it–Montezuma's Revenge. About two days out from our goal, La Paz, Cam came down with it. Privacy now became a much lower priority. She'd just grab her roll of toilet paper and dash behind the truck.

But by the time we reached La Paz, she was in fine shape.

We checked into a hotel, and for the first time in two weeks we slept on a real mattress, cleaned up under a real shower, and ate food other than tortillas, beans, and Dinty Moore stew.

We put the truck onto a ferry and rode across the Gulf of California to mainland Mexico where a paved highway took us north to the U. S. border in two days.

Driving the Baja was truly an unforgettable odyssey, certainly risky, downright dangerous if you were careless or unlucky. But one thing will always stick in my mind. We didn't encounter many other drivers on that awful road, but when we did they never just passed us by. Mexicans and Americans alike would always stop and ask: Are you doing okay? Any problems with your truck? Do you need any gas? How's your supply of beer? We have extra. One time when we were stuck in the sand a Mexican man driving an old clunker came along. Without a word he jumped out with his spade and pitched right in to get us going again. The people were just great. And it was contagious. Soon we were doing the same thing–trying to help others. My Spanish improved a lot and so did my outlook on life.

If that road was still unpaved would I make the trip today? Not likely. Mexico, with its drug wars, has unfortunately become a much different place.

ATTEMPTS AT THE NORTH POLE

The North Pole is located in the middle of the Arctic Ocean on an extensive floating icecap that expands in winter and contracts in summer. It's in total darkness for much of the year, but by April daylight lasts for twenty-four-hours, continuing throughout the summer. If you're inclined to travel to the North Pole, April is the best month, given the constant daylight and relatively stable temperature (twenty below zero Fahrenheit) to keep the ice firm.

But it's no trip to Disneyland. Besides the brutal cold, there are other problems. Pressure ridges formed by buckling ice can reach heights of thirty feet or more and have to be climbed over with heavy loads of equipment and supplies. Open channels of water lie across your path, stretching for long distances. They have to be either crossed–very tricky and dangerous–or skirted around, adding extra miles to the journey. Finally, the ice itself frequently drifts southward. You can walk fifteen miles a day toward the Pole and drift back ten.

So why am I bringing all this up? Don't laugh now, but I've attempted to reach the North Pole three times.

I'm not kidding. But I wouldn't have tried it on foot–that's for certifiable lunatics–but rather by air.

In 1992 I paid a large sum of money to an arctic exploration outfit to fly me to the North Pole and land on the ice in a small plane outfitted with skis. At the time it sounded like a painless way to stand on the Pole, hold up a flag, get my picture taken wearing a sappy grin, and later be able to say that *I DID IT*!

It didn't work out as planned. The pilot of the small Twin Otter plane circled the Pole at very low altitude, but the thick bank of fog went right down to the polar ice so we couldn't land. I chalked up the venture as a ridiculous middle-age attempt to recapture my youth and went back to my sane, mundane, paper-shuffling, workaday world.

Yet I'd become friends with Skip Vorhees, the owner of the exploration company, and one night in April '94 he called me.

"Wanna go on a North Pole trip?" he asked.

"I tried that, remember? Are you falling behind on your house payments again and need some quick cash?"

"This time it's free."

"Free?"

"Yep. I can't make the trip this year and I need a group leader."

My responsibility would be to meet with the paying clients at the beginning of the excursion, inspect their clothing so they wouldn't charge out onto the frozen tundra wearing leather dress gloves instead of wool-lined mitts, explain to them that polar bears, not humans, were at the top of the arctic food chain, and then shepherd them from one stopover point to the next.

Unfortunately, the group leader's job description didn't guarantee actually *going* to the North Pole. The final 690-mile leg from Eureka–a Canadian weather station on the eightieth parallel–to the Pole required that the plane carry a huge load of fuel and the group leader was extraneous weight and would not be aboard for the last segment to the Pole.

However, many of the clients came from warm climates, and if even one of them chickened out at the last minute after getting a taste of a minus-sixty-degree wind chill, it would lighten the plane and I'd have another shot at the Pole.

"When do I leave?" I asked.

Sadly for me all the clients hung in there, and on the day they traveled to the Pole I waited for their return at the weather station, passing time by throwing food scraps to the white arctic fox that came begging at the kitchen door.

The following year I got another call from Vorhees.

"I've only got four clients this year–plenty of room for the group leader to ride all the way to the Pole. Interested?"

Was he kidding? "When do I leave?" I asked in a restrained voice.

I met the four men at Edmonton, Alberta and we headed north, making stops at high arctic Inuit (Eskimo) villages before winding up at the Eureka weather station on 21 April.

Even *flying* to the Pole isn't without its problems. The Twin Otter doesn't have enough range to make the final leg nonstop, so the small arctic airline company deposits drums of fuel on the icecap at around the 87th parallel (200 miles from the Pole)–an unmanned, self-service gas station, if you will. The strategy is to put the plane down on the icecap at this unmanned fuel cache, refuel, and continue on to the Pole.

But this refueling can be tricky. To land anywhere on the icecap, the weather and the ice have to be almost perfect. An overcast sky can produce what's called "flat light," preventing the pilot from using shadows to distinguish any roughness in the ice that could damage the landing gear, or worse, crack up the airplane. This is *not* the place to have an accident.

The morning of the twenty-second was bright and clear at Eureka, and the adrenalin was running high as we took off from the airstrip on the 1380-mile round trip flight to the North Pole. It looked good.

Good, that is, until we got about twenty miles south of the fuel cache where thick cloud cover cut off the sunlight, producing the flat-light condition.

But the fuel cache site had been used several times recently and the pilot knew that the ice had been pretty smooth. After circling around the drums at low altitude for one last inspection, he brought the plane in for a landing.

The Otter hit the ice like a barrel of bricks. It began pitching and rolling crazily as it skittered and banged along the icecap. Ten seconds later we finally bounced to a stop. After thousands of airplane landings, I suddenly knew the value of a seat belt–it keeps you from flying about the cabin.

A polar storm occurring a few days before had blown snow across the marked landing area at the fuel cache, forming two-foot-high drifts that were virtually invisible from the air, especially in flat light. Extreme cold hardened the drifts so that the Otter's landing skis bounced off rather than going through them.

Instead of coming back into the cabin to reassure us that everything was okay, the pilot stepped out of his cockpit door and grabbed a shovel from the plane's luggage compartment, dourly motioning for us to get out of the plane.

"The first order of business is to clear a strip so we can get this plane off the ice again," he said soberly. He stared out into the icy wind, the direction he wanted to take off into, and with the shovel quickly began to chop the nearest snow drift into chunks like he was going to build an igloo.

"How long a strip do you need?" I asked him.

"Five hundred feet."

Five hundred feet is nothing at an airport, but five hundred feet on the polar icecap filled with hardened snow drifts that had to be removed piecemeal was a long, long way.

With the pilot carving up the snow into chunks, the rest of us diligently followed along behind, furiously throwing or carrying the pieces off to one side. The wind chill factor was a bracing thirty-five below zero, and this fact alone made our runway-building very efficient. The prospect of freezing to death if we took a break kept us moving.

"Are you going to refuel when we get this done?" I asked the pilot.

"I don't think it's a good idea. With a full load of fuel, we'd need almost a thousand feet to get the plane in the air."

I looked at the runway we were laboring on, perhaps two hundred feet cleared and *that* didn't look all that great. The construction crew–myself; Amy, the female copilot from Ontario; a plant nursery-store owner from Long Island; a missile engineer from Alabama; a psychiatrist from Nashville; and a system analyst from Baltimore–was beginning to stagger from exhaustion.

"Five hundred feet it is," I said licking at the icicles growing from my mustache.

After an hour and a half when we just about had the job done, the wind shifted ninety degrees.

"Taking off from this stuff in a crosswind is bad," the pilot said. "I think we'd better build another runway."

"How about a control tower while we're at it?" I suggested. No one laughed.

After three hours on the icecap we finished the second runway and scrambled into the plane before the wind changed direction again. The pilot looked at the portly psychiatrist from Nashville. "Would you mind sitting in the rear of the cabin? I have to get the nose of the plane up quickly on takeoff."

With both engines screaming, the Otter bounced along our homemade runway and leapt into the air. We headed south. Without the extra fuel, we had to return to the Eureka weather station.

But fortune appeared to smile on us that night. A five-man

British expedition walking to the Pole had made a distress call to Eureka. They needed a medical evacuation for one of their party. After several phone calls it was determined that by splitting the fuel cost between us and the British sponsors, we could get another try at the Pole. However, the airline people had put the fuel cache site off limits due to the dangerous landing conditions. They decided to load as many 55-gallon fuel drums into the Otter as possible, fly to the North Pole nonstop, refuel the plane from the drums when they landed, and pick up the British evacuee on the return trip.

The next morning our pilot came up to me in the Eureka dining room during breakfast. "With all those fuel drums aboard, I can only take four people maximum without exceeding the plane's payload capacity."

The four clients with me had paid thousands of dollars apiece to get to the North Pole. I had paid nothing, so there was no question who was going to be the odd man out. I just couldn't believe it was happening to me again.

So while the clients and pilots flew to the Pole on their dual mission, I again hung around the weather station, grumbling about the rotten hand that fate had once more dealt me.

After dinner I was still feeling morose when I looked out a window and spotted a white arctic wolf standing about twenty feet from the front door. I grabbed my camera and snapped his picture before he trotted off. My spirits lifted and I had to tell someone.

John MacIver, one of the weather analysts I had gotten to know, was in the station's rec room sipping a glass of home-made beer that they brewed at the station during the long winter nights. I told him about the wolf.

"Yeah, there's been a lot of 'em around here lately-pretty tame too," he replied. "Every once in awhile a few of the guys tie a wiener on the end of some fishing line and cast it out onto the ice. Sometimes a wolf'll chase the wiener when you reel it back in." He chuckled. "It's a lot of fun, even the wolf enjoys it."

It was an outrageous story and I didn't know whether to believe him or not. It could be true; people get a little strange after they've been up in the arctic awhile. I thought *I'm* getting a little strange. I've been up there three times now and have yet to stand on the North Pole. But for some reason I keep coming back. Maybe it's flying over Ellsmere Island's majestically stark mountains covered with blue-white ice and snow, where no man has set foot and hopefully never will. Maybe it's the people who live and work up here, taking on the frightening elements with casualness, patience, and biting humor. Maybe it's the wolf, unconcernedly standing out by the front door, looking right at home because, after all, he *is* at home.

Will I try it again if I get asked? I'll say, "When do I leave?" I really don't expect too much anymore. It'll just be an all-expense-paid trip to the eightieth parallel. Next time maybe I'll take up fishing for wolves.

YELLOWKNIFE

In the summer of 1975 the *Los Angeles Times* ran a small article stating that in the community of Yellowknife in northern Canada the men sent their wives south for the winter to keep them from committing suicide.

"Suicide?" I exclaimed, reading the article over my morning coffee. "There's actually a place so desolate that residents want to commit suicide? I've got to check this out!"

The story triggered a bizarre quirk in my psyche. I experience an unexplainable need to take vacations in places where no one else wants to go.

I knew nothing about Yellowknife, so I began doing some research. I bought a map of Canada and checked out books from the local library.

The city of Yellowknife is the capital of the Northwest Territories of Canada. In 1975 the population was 6000 people. Half of the people were Caucasians who worked in government offices, and the other half were mixed races. The community lies on the northwestern shore of the Great

Slave Lake, one of the larger lakes on the North American continent, 250 miles south of the Arctic Circle and over 1000 miles north of the U. S./Canadian border. Winters in Yellowknife are cold, the average January temperature being -17 degrees F.

In the 1890's a Klondike-bound prospector made a discovery of gold in the Great Slave Lake area. However, the finding was largely ignored because of the Klondike gold rush in the Northwest Territory of Canada and the extreme remoteness of the Great Slave Lake region.

It wasn't until the early 1930's with more gold discoveries that Yellowknife became a village largely occupied by prospectors.

With the establishment of two large gold mines Yellowknife had a mini-boom in 1938 with new businesses coming in, including the Canadian Bank of Commerce, a hotel, drug store, pool hall and a post office.

With more gold mines opening, Yellowknife steadily grew, and in 1967 it became the capital of the Northwest Territories of Canada. The population expanded further with the forming of government offices.

In 1975 the Yellowknife economy still consisted largely of the Northwest Territories provincial government and the gold mines. The major flow of commerce between Yellowknife and the rest of Canada was by air. The building of a decent highway up to the Great Slave Lake area on permafrost was prohibitively expensive.

There was a road of sorts connecting northern Alberta to Yellowknife mostly to accommodate trucks hauling supplies not easily or economically transported by air. This road was graded dirt and gravel–two ruts in places–and over 500 miles long. Tourists were advised not to drive the road, not only because of its poor condition, but the drive also posed a risk due to lack of gas stations and other facilities.

I got excited thinking of a drive along that road. Four years earlier I had driven the treacherous dirt road that ran the length of Baja California and I'd had the time of my life.

I mentioned the Yellowknife trip to my girlfriend, Cam, who'd gone with me down the Baja. Without hesitation she accepted.

I also invited my good friend, Ralph Manus, to come along. He said, "Why not?'

This trip posed one unique problem that I hadn't encountered in the Baja. Mosquitoes.

We were planning to go in late August, before the cold weather set in. From previous summer trips into western Canada I'd had first-hand encounters with Canadian mosquitoes and it wasn't a pleasant experience. The shell on the back of my Chevy pickup wasn't going to keep them out.

When I was married to my second wife, Jo Ann, we'd bought a 20-foot Prowler travel trailer that we used extensively on summer vacations. After the divorce in 1970 I sold the trailer but now realized that the Prowler would be just the thing for the Yellowknife trip. It had a bed, couch, butane stove and a bathroom complete with shower.

I contacted the present owner of the trailer, and we

struck a four-week rental agreement. But I was to find out that taking the Prowler to Yellowknife would turn out to be a costly venture.

In the third week in August I hooked the Prowler up to my Chevy pickup, and the three of us headed north from Los Angeles. Three days later we crossed the northern U. S. border into Canada. Picking up more supplies in Calgary, we continued north.

We hit the outskirts of Edmonton, then turned northwest past the Lesser Slave Lake to Peace River, the last town of any appreciable size we'd see before reaching Yellowknife. Turning directly north again we traveled through a few tiny villages, and 180 miles north of Peace River reached the small outpost of High Level, the end of the pavement. Now, I thought, the trip would get interesting.

We spent the night in High Level parked alongside a town road. Thick clouds of large mosquitoes angrily banged against the Prowler window screens, trying to get at our flesh. We were thankful for the safety of the trailer.

The next morning we pulled out onto the gravel-covered dirt road to Yellowknife. An hour later we noticed a large ball of dust off ahead of us.

"What's that?" Cam asked.

I shook my head. "I dunno. But whatever it is it's coming right at us."

When the giant dust ball was about 200 yards in front of us, the grill of a Mack truck emerged out of the dust. I quickly put on the brakes.

The gravel road was narrow, and the large truck came within inches of tearing off my side mirror. The blast of dust-laden air being carried along violently rocked the pickup and the Prowler. Flying rocks pelted us.

We sat there for a long moment, gathering our wits.

"You think we're going to run into many of those?" Ralph asked.

I put the pickup into gear and slowly moved ahead. "I don't know. I hope not."

But we did. Every half hour or so a dust dragon–that's what we called them–would appear and roar past us.

The pickup and trailer were suffering rock damage from the passing trucks. I was particularly concerned about the trailer because it was no longer mine. Several holes had been punched into the aluminum left side of the Prowler. A small grocery store in the settlement of Indian Cabins gave me some empty cardboard boxes which I flattened and taped to the trailer, but much of the damage had already been done.

Late in the day we pulled into Hay River, a small remote outpost near the south shore of the Great Slave Lake. There were campsites available with electrical and sewage hookups, so we pulled into a site and connected up.

I thought that the mosquitoes were bad south of here, but we hadn't seen anything yet. Hay River mosquitoes were major league. Multiple layers of repellant kept them mostly at bay, but I was still getting covered with red welts whenever the swarms discovered any untreated bare spots.

Hay River had a bar/restaurant which we literally ran to,

trying to get away from the ugly black clouds of mosquitoes. We sat down in a booth and ordered beers.

The lone waitress, menus in hand, explained that since it was Sunday we could only get alcoholic beverages if we also ordered food. The reason was that the Canadian government didn't want anyone getting drunk on Sunday, and food would keep you sober.

That was fine, we said, we were going to eat anyway. So we ordered food from the menu and got our beer.

Two whiskered men in dirty plaid shirts–obviously locals–came in and sat at a nearby table. The waitress wordlessly put a shot of whiskey and a beer in front of each of them. By the time we got our food these two were working on their third round of drinks.

The waitress brought two steaming plates of food to the drinkers. Hot turkey sandwiches, heaps of mashed potatoes, string beans, all swimming in gravy. She also placed a paper shopping bag lined with waxed paper on the floor between their chairs and then went back to the kitchen.

The two locals tipped their plates of food into the shopping bag, slopping in the contents and then proceeded with their drinking. They'd eat their food later, but no goofy law was going to keep them from their primary mission of getting drunk.

The next morning we headed out, traveling around the west end of the Great Slave Lake. We were still a ways from Yellowknife.

It was a bumpy, dusty ride, and dodging oncoming trucks

was a nerve-wracking job. There were Yellowknife-bound trucks passing us, but those encounters weren't nearly as frightening as the ones coming toward us.

The trees were getting smaller, and although it was still August there was a definite chill in the air.

A day later we arrived in Yellowknife. I looked around as we drove through town. After anticipating this moment for months I was disappointed. In 1975 Yellowknife was a somewhat dumpy little burg. Loose dogs roamed the streets, some of them chasing cars. Small old clapboard houses with peeling paint were scattered alongside the cracked, potholed streets; no doubt the homes of gold miners. Some of the little houses were merely covered with tar paper. A group of stucco single-story buildings housed the Northwest Territories government offices.

A newer five-story structure was a hotel–by far the tallest building in Yellowknife. I pulled into the hotel parking lot. After nearly two weeks of living in the cramped quarters of the trailer, Cam and I were more than ready to enjoy the comfort of hotel accommodations.

But it wasn't going to be that hotel. I went up to the front desk. Yes, they had rooms available; for $125 a night.

$125 a *NIGHT??* That was Canadian money, of course, but still out of my price range. Remember, this was 1975.

The clerk recommended that we might want to consider the Gold Hotel down the street which was more modestly priced.

The Gold wasn't really a hotel. It was a group of small

pre-fab buildings looking like they dated back to World War II. One of them was the front office.

The hotel owner allowed us to look inside one of the units. It wasn't much; cracked linoleum on the floor, old peeling wallpaper, about seventeen coats of enamel on the old dresser. But the unit was much larger than the trailer, and the price was right so we took it. Ralph would have the Prowler all to himself.

Down the street was a decent-looking restaurant, so we went there for dinner, and we all enjoyed the locally caught salmon.

Our server was an elderly fellow with a Scottish accent. Ralph asked him if Yellowknife had a nice cocktail lounge where we could get an after-dinner drink. The server mentioned a few places, but then leaned over and said in a whisper, "But ye wanna stay away from the Trapline Bar. It's a rough and ready place."

"Where is the Trapline Bar?" I asked. "We should know where it is so we can stay away from it."

We left the restaurant. Nothing would do but Ralph and I had to check out the Trapline Bar. Cam wasn't interested in a rough and ready place and went back to the "hotel room." She was keeping a journal of our trip and every evening logged in our daily activities.

The Trapline Bar had fur pelts, pelt stretchers, and steel scissor traps mounted on the walls. Old wooden chairs previously broken were crudely patched together. The wooden tables were deeply scarred with initials of knife-wielding patrons. The room was thick with cigarette smoke. Country music blared from a single speaker.

The customers were all dark-skinned men, most of them aboriginal and others with Oriental features, all burly and mean-looking. They were gold miners coming off their shift. Two waitresses busily circulated among the tables serving up shots and beers, the drink combination of choice.

A black man was sitting at a table by himself, drinking 7-UP. Drinking *7-UP?* How odd!

Ralph and I took stools at the bar, ordered beer, and began watching the other drinkers.

An hour passed and the voices in the room got louder, shouting in languages I'd never heard. The crowd was getting rowdy, but the black man just sat there drinking his 7-UP.

Suddenly two guys jumped to their feet and began punching each other in the head. I'd seen plenty of fist fights in the movies but never the real thing. Beer glasses fell to the floor and smashed.

The 7-UP drinker jumped to his feet, ran over to the fight, grabbed one of the combatants by the back of his shirt, hoisted him up on his tiptoes and marched him over to the door. The bartender, with a practiced move, hurried over to the door and opened it. The brawler was tossed out onto the street.

The other fighter stood next to his overturned chair, looking fiercely at no one in particular. The black man strode over to him and jerked his thumb toward the door.

The fighter, blood leaking from his nose, glared at him

and barked profanities in a strange language. Then he thought better of whatever he intended to do and walked out the door. The bouncer sat back down at his table and picked up his 7-UP. A waitress swept up the broken glass and mopped up the blood spots on the floor.

Ten minutes later another fight broke out. The bouncer got up again and trotted over to two men who were slapping each other around. One of the fighters–the larger one–broke off the fight and lunged at the black man, giant fists swinging in wild arcs.

Big mistake. The bouncer dodged the fists and delivered a swift jab to the big man's jaw, dropping him to the floor.

The drinking crowd loved it, clapping and cheering despite the fact that the loser was one of their own.

Ralph and I watched two more fights, but when it was obvious that the outcome wasn't about to change we decided to leave.

Cam had an interesting evening of her own. She had been in the bathroom sitting on the toilet, happily entering our day's activities in her journal when she heard the door of our rented unit open.

"Rosie? Are you here? Where are you?"

Two young guys appeared at the bathroom door. "Yer not Rosie. Where's Rosie?"

It seemed that Rosie had been the previous occupant of the pre-fab rental unit, and she had entertained a lot of the gold miners, for a fee, of course.

Cam stood up and pulled up her panties. She explained

that Rosie didn't live there anymore and that they better leave.

One of them said, "Whadda *YOU* charge?"

Cam threw them out.

We hung around Yellowknife for a couple of days to see the sights but soon found out that there were no more sights to see. I was interested in looking at the workings of a gold mine, but security was so high that we couldn't get within 300 yards of any mine operations. Then we decided to enjoy the scenery along the Great Slave Lake, but the shoreline looked like the location of an Alfred Hitchcock movie with slate-gray water lashing up at scraggly evergreen trees. Finally we opted to head back to sunny Southern California.

The journey back would turn out to be one of the most interesting parts of the trip if you can classify high anxiety as interesting.

On the morning of 31 August we prepared to leave. It was so cold that I was wearing a sheepskin coat while hitching the trailer to the pickup truck. We rolled south out of town with the truck heater blasting hot air. Hay River was 300 miles from Yellowknife, and we were hoping to reach it by day's end.

Again we encountered the large trucks, this time heading to Yellowknife, and again we endured showers of rocks as they passed.

About 50 miles south of Yellowknife I noticed steam billowing out from beneath the truck's hood. I glanced at the water-temperature gauge. It was right on H.

I pulled over, opened the hood, and with rag in hand

carefully opened the radiator cap. Steam and water gushed out. I immediately saw the problem. On the way to Yellowknife we had stopped for gas at one of the few-and-far-between gas stations on the gravel stretch above Hi Level. The station sold grill screens to prevent rocks from flying in through the grill and damaging the radiator. I had bought one and attached it to the front of the truck's grill.

The screen worked fine on the northbound trip, but that morning on the way back a very large sharp rock had penetrated the screen and punched a hole in the radiator core. Radiator fluid was flowing out.

Fortunately we had filled the water tank in the trailer that morning, and we had plenty of water for the radiator, or so we thought.

We each grabbed containers from the Prowler's cupboards, filled them with water and emptied them into the radiator. We were on our way again.

But thirty minutes later the temp gauge was again heading toward H. I pulled over and took a closer look at the leak. It was worse that I had originally thought. We filled the radiator again.

A half hour later we had to stop again. This time when we were in the trailer, filling containers with water Ralph began filling himself with Red Mountain white wine ($1.65 a gallon) that we'd brought along from California.

And so it went. Every half hour we'd stop and fill the radiator with water, and Ralph would fill up with wine. The situation was really worrying him, but it was also worrying me. And Cam, a smoker, was now lighting up each cigarette from the butt of the last one.

After three hours we arrived at a small burg with a gas station. I bought a can of radiator sealant and poured it in.

The sealant didn't work. We continued having to stop frequently, pouring water into the radiator. A couple of hours later after several stops we pulled up at the next small gas station. I bought a different brand of radiator sealant and poured that in.

That sealant didn't do the job either. It was now late in the afternoon, and we were still a long way from Hay River, so I pulled over into a clearing and made camp. Water was now at a premium so there was no washing up, only wine with meals and no teeth brushing.

Early morning on the second day out we hit the road again. Finally, after another day of filling the radiator every half hour in the boondocks, we reached Hay River, which now seemed like a cosmopolitan center. We pulled into the same campground where we had spent the night on the way up to Yellowknife and hooked up. Our salvation was the fact that we had access to water.

Before filling up the trailer water tank we took turns taking showers. We didn't know when we'd have the opportunity to take another one.

The next morning I bought a third brand of radiator solvent at the Hay River gas station and uttered a silent prayer that this one would do the job. I also picked up another radiator screen and attached it over the first one. The last thing we needed was another hole in the radiator core. We were still 200 miles from High Level, Alberta, the beginning of paved highway.

I did a mental calculation of how long it would take to get back to Los Angeles if we had to stop every half hour to fill the radiator. The three of us were scheduled to report to work the next Monday, and we weren't going to make it with the radiator in its present condition.

Around noon we pulled up at the first gas station below Hay River. I noticed that they had yet another brand of radiator sealant. Hope springs eternal and I bought a can.

I opened the can, looked inside, and showed it to Cam.

"What is that?" she asked.

"It's supposed to be radiator sealant."

"Radiator sealant? It looks like cooked beets. How are you supposed to get it into the radiator?"

"I dunno. Just cram it in, I guess."

And that's what I did. The water in the radiator seemed to dissolve the "cooked beets" and I managed to get the entire can of sealant into the radiator.

And it worked! We got back to Los Angeles, and the water temperature never reached H. In fact, I kept the Chevy pickup for another twenty years and sold it with the original radiator core.

I had to settle up financially with the Prowler owner to cover the rock damage. My pickup had lots of rock dings in the left side. I had to have the truck repaired and repainted.

In 1975 Yellowknife certainly wasn't a tourist attraction,

but as I mentioned, I got a perverse pleasure going to places where you couldn't be sure you were going to make it back.

One time in the mid 1990's I had occasion to be in Yellowknife on a three hour airport layover. I hired a cab to take a quick look around the city. I didn't recognize the place! Yellowknife is now a very upscale provincial capital. The gold mines are closed now, but diamonds have been discovered, and the local economy is flourishing.

I asked the cabbie about the Trapline Bar. He'd never heard of it.

I didn't ask but I suppose that they'd paved the road to High Level. Too bad.

HELSINKI

I n 1999 I took a Baltic cruise, touring the larger Northern European cities; Copenhagen, Oslo, Stockholm, Helsinki, St. Petersburg, and Tallin, Estonia. I scarfed up untold quantities of pickled herring, smoked salmon, Danish cheese and lingonberry pie. The shops I was in featured endless racks of hand-knit Nordic ski sweaters, herds of plush stuffed reindeer, and armies of troll dolls. I rubbed elbows with more Lutherans than one would ever expect to meet in a lifetime.

Since I'm a Finnish American, I want to share some of my observations on Helsinki in 1999.

When Yoopers claim that summer occurs on the Fourth of July, it's said with tongue in cheek. In Finland it's pretty much true. The morning I arrived in Helsinki–16 August–the temperature was in the low fifties–not too bad–but it didn't get much warmer. Only a few weeks earlier the sandy beaches near the city were filled with sun-bronzed Finns. By mid-August they were deserted. Summer in Finland was over. By mid August it was too cold to go to the beach.

Finland has had a long history of lengthy occupation by other countries, yet current-day Helsinki–population 600,000–is a bustling, self-sufficient, beautiful city. With an innate artistry which seemingly runs contrary to their stern, sisu-like nature, the Finns have skillfully woven streets around and through dense groves of birch trees and rock-bluff outcroppings. Parks abound. Electric streetcars glide along the wide, clean downtown boulevards. There's moderate traffic congestion, but no horn honking or short-tempers. Road rage is beneath the dignity of Helsinki drivers. Mannerheimintie, the major avenue named after a Finnish military leader and statesman, is most cosmopolitan with large, up-scale stores, including Stockman's, a Baltic replica of Harrod's in London.

Many people aren't aware that Finland is officially bilingual. Swedes occupied the country for so many centuries that both languages are commonly used, making the reading of Helsinki street signs, with their fifteen-plus-letter Finnish and Swedish names, a real job.

But it's actually quite easy for Americans to explore Helsinki since practically everyone speaks English. In fact, the Finns speak a lot of languages. In addition to Finnish and Swedish, English and German are compulsory in the elementary schools.

Most Helsinki restaurants will provide you with an English-language menu on request. However, if you're still unsure of the food there are plenty of McDonald's and Pizza

Huts around to see you through. Visa and Mastercard are widely accepted, even by taxicab drivers. Many stores will also accept American money if you don't mind getting your change in Finnmarks.

Speaking of money, bring lots of it. At a small downtown café I had a modest lunch consisting of a smoked-salmon-and-cheese sandwich, a small piece of lingonberry pie, and a cup of coffee. The bill came to the equivalent of fourteen dollars. A cup of coffee costs two dollars, and if you want a refill it's another dollar. Remember, this was 1999. I don't even want to think what these prices would be today. On the upside, tipping is not expected.

At Stockman's–admittedly a pricey store–men's shirts went for ninety dollars. Neckties, fifty. A plain-Jane, three-cushion sofa costs the equivalent of two thousand U.S. dollars.

In the city proper there are almost no single-family homes available, so the Finns buy apartments. Now we're talking *real* money. A cozy two-bedroom apartment (600-700 sq ft–I mean *small*) will set you back 800,000 to 1 million Finnmarks, or 150-200,000 U.S. dollars. Remember again, this was 1999.

Taxes are stiff. Hard merchandise has a 22% value-added tax (VAT), driving up the price of clothing, furniture, housing and automobiles. Even the churches (86% Lutheran) get into the tax act. The government nicks everyone's paycheck with a one-percent church tax. Books are tax exempt, though. Finns believe that literature is a necessity and should be available to all at minimum cost.

On a new automobile (all of them are imported) the import tax is an incredible 130 percent, driving the cost of an unadorned Chevy van well over $50,000 U.S. (1999 prices). But you'd never buy a Chevy van anyway. Gasoline runs about four dollars a gallon, and only the most affluent motorists can afford to drive big cars with V-8 or V-6 engines.

With this very high cost of living, it's no small wonder that Finns ferry across the Gulf of Finland to Estonia to do their shopping.

But they endure. The economy is strong, unemployment is minimal, and they somehow managed to avoid becoming embroiled in the insanity of world politics.

In 1999 Helsinki residents were sporting caps and T-shirts reading "Helsinki 450," advertising the city's four-hundred and fiftieth birthday in the year 2000.

I can highly recommend a trip to Helsinki. Just bring lots of money.

ONE SCARY AIRPLANE RIDE

During my lifetime I've flown a couple of thousand times. I don't enjoy the flying experience anymore, but not because I'm worried about the plane falling out of the sky. I worry about missing my connection in Detroit. I hate it when the plane is sitting at the gate, and the pilot announces that there'll be a delay because one of the lavatories is malfunctioning, and FAA regulations dictate that he can't take off until it's fixed. My stomach really churns when the six-year-old son of Satan sitting behind me kicks the back of my seat 5000 times between Chicago and Los Angeles.

I shouldn't complain about these situations, though. I once took an airplane ride where there was a much better reason for my stomach to churn.

In 1958 my first wife, Emily, and I were living in Los Angeles. We had scraped up enough money to fly down to Mexico City for a short vacation. The cheapest fare I could find was a Mexicana Airlines red eye flight leaving LA at

10PM and reaching Mexico City in the morning. We were flying a DC-6, a four-engine piston-driven workhorse of the airlines before jets were introduced.

Emily fell asleep shortly after we took off, but I was too wired with anticipation of the trip.

Back then the airlines felt that it was a good idea to keep passengers in a tranquil state of mind, so they handed out as many complementary drinks as you wanted. I ordered a beer and struck up a conversation with another American tourist sitting across the aisle. Two hours and several beers later we were both rather "tranquil" when I noticed a bright, flickering light outside the darkened window. An engine was on fire.

"Hey, look at that," I said to my beery friend.

He glanced out the window. "How about that? I wonder if the pilot knows. Say, don't we need another beer?"

I woke Emily up to show her the engine fire. She took one look out the window and began screaming.

My friend across the aisle tapped me and said, "Better tell your wife to keep it down. There's people trying to sleep in here."

I was considerably more sober by the time we made an emergency landing on a gravel runway at Mazatlan. Everyone was herded off the plane, and sleepy airport workers hosed down the smoking engine. No one informed us what was going to happen next, so we stood around on the edge of the runway and waited.

Before long another Mexicana DC-6 approached and landed, and the passengers–working-class Mexican citizens–

were directed to get off. As soon as the newly arrived plane was vacated, our planeload of Los Angeles tourists were told to get on. We boarded the new DC-6 and proceeded on to Mexico City. Mexicana Airlines really knew how to take care of their American tourists, yet I've often wondered what happened to the Mexican nationals who got left standing at the Mazlatan airport runway at three in the morning.

MY DESOTO MOTOR-HOME

Summer is the fun season when everyone hits the road and goes camping. For many, however, modern-day camping is a far cry from heating pork and beans over an open fire and curling up in a sleeping bag beneath the stars. Nowadays, a lot of people choose to buy a motor home, for example. Most of these behemoths–price tags well into six figures–have expandable living rooms, large-screen TV's, microwave ovens, dishwashers, king-size beds, and Jacuzzis. This is camping?

I once owned a motor home. A DeSoto. Never heard of a DeSoto motor home, you say? Well, I had one. In 1958 I was newly married and working as a junior engineer at Douglas Aircraft in Santa Monica, California. My bride, Emily, was a student at UCLA with zero income. In those days we were so financially strapped that if a wolf had come to our door we'd have eaten it.

But every weekend we'd strike out from our tiny apartment in search of adventure because our hearts were young and gay. (This was back in the days when gay had a different meaning.)

That summer we bought a 1947 DeSoto for $250. The car had an asthmatic engine, bald tires, and Chrysler's early experimental version of fluid drive which took about a minute or so after you pressed the gas pedal for it to realize that you wanted to go forward.

But the DeSoto had one very attractive feature. Room. It was an old limousine with a pair of jump seats in the rear. When the seats were folded up you could easily sleep two across on the rear floor. This was our motor home.

One weekend we decided to explore Mexicali, a Mexican border town out in the desert across from the city of Calexico on the California side. We loaded up the DeSoto with pillows, blankets (sleeping bags weren't in our budget), groceries, and beer. The plan was to explore Mexico and then come back to Calexico, find a nice secluded town park, and camp for the night in our cozy motor home.

Such was the plan.

Everything was going just swell until about midnight when we began looking for a campsite. There weren't any parks in Calexico, only dark, dusty streets with suspicious characters skulking along the sidewalks. We proceeded out of town and wound up on an unpaved road. There were no trees, only sand and sagebrush and a bad smell that we couldn't identify. I decided to turn around, but the road was too narrow, so I drove on, searching for a wide spot. We finally came up on an expanse of hardpan. The smell was getting worse.

I backed the DeSoto out onto the hardpan to turn around. But when I got all four wheels onto it, the heavy limo broke through a sun-baked two-inch crust. We sunk into what turned out to be the entire sewage output from the city of Calexico. Our motor home was up to the axles in a sea of poop.

I put the DeSoto in forward, then reverse, trying to rock loose, but the wheels just went ZZZZZZZ, sending up a thick spray of you-know-what.

Every flying insect in the state of California and all the northern provinces of Mexico smelled the result and zeroed in on us. My wife began moaning piteously.

I had no shovel, but there was a small metal panel in the trunk which had fallen off from somewhere on the car, so I began using it in a futile attempt to dig us out. The bugs went insane with glee. Emily was sitting in the limo, loudly questioning the wisdom of agreeing to be my bride.

By and by, headlights appeared along the road. A Border Patrol officer in a jeep pulled up and shone a flashlight on us, thinking that we were illegals crossing over from Mexico.

When he saw our blonde heads he asked, "What in the world are you people doing out here? Do you know what this is?"

We explained our situation and that, yes, we now had a pretty good idea what it was that we were in. He had a good laugh over that and then told us that he'd pull us out. He got in his jeep and began backing out onto the hardpan to attach a cable to the front of the DeSoto.

"Don't drive onto it," I cried. "You'll break through like we did!"

He turned and looked at me, laughing heartily. "Don't worry. I've got four-wheel drive."

His jeep did, in fact, break through the crust, but the officer wasn't troubled at all. He attached a steel cable to the front of the DeSoto. We both got into our vehicles, put them in gear, and stomped on the gas pedals.

Six wheels going ZZZZZZZ can churn up a lot more poop than two wheels. The four-wheel-drive jeep dug itself in even deeper than the DeSoto. Being behind the jeep, my windshield instantly turned dark brown, along with the hood, grill and front fenders. The bugs were now inviting their relatives in from Nevada, Arizona, and New Mexico. My wife's moaning had turned into a shrill screech.

The Border Patrol officer no longer saw any humor in the situation. In fact, he'd become downright grumpy. He got on his two-way radio and began barking at someone at the Border Patrol headquarters. Soon another jeep appeared.

"Don't drive out on this stuff!" the first officer yelled at the new arrival.

With the second jeep remaining on the road, we hooked the three vehicles in tandem and churned away. Slowly but surely, through a brown blizzard, my DeSoto motor home rose out of the poop lagoon. It was not a pretty sight.

The two officers told us to get out of there and never darken their border again. In the early morning light we took off for Los Angeles. The limo was filthy and the smell was horrific. Palm trees wilted along the highway as we passed. It was hard to navigate because the wipers were glued to the windshield.

That was my first and last motor home. I sold the DeSoto soon afterward. I don't remember who bought it, but as I recall, I had the buyer standing upwind of the vehicle until the deal was closed.

LIFE AND DEATH IN THE BIG EASY

Years ago I took a trip to New Orleans to find out why it has such a seamy reputation. I made the mistake of going in late June.

Summer isn't exactly the high-tourist season in the Big Easy. I realized this as I was sitting in my room at the downtown Holiday Inn wringing out my socks. In fact, and I'm not making this up, New Orleans is ranked as the third "sweatiest city" in the country, based on the average summertime temperature and humidity. If the alligators were smart they'd crawl out of the swamps and migrate north in July and August.

Speaking of swamps, New Orleans is the only city where you can plunk down money to have someone take you on a tour of a swamp. That's right, you can go eyeball to eyeball with a Louisiana gator while squadrons of musclebound mosquitoes attempt to lift you out of the boat and carry you off. Sounds like great fun, eh? Needless to say, I didn't take the tour.

One popular New Orleans tourist highlight is a visit to one of its world-famous cemeteries. Most of the city is at or below sea level, which makes in-ground burials out of the question due to the very shallow water table. Therefore, the cemeteries are filled with grandiose above-ground mausoleums. Less prosperous inhabitants are interred in small public niches resembling baker's ovens stacked upon one another.

The larger tombs are family vaults with literally dozens of names engraved on them, some dating back to the eighteenth century. The vaults are large, but not *that* large, begging the question, how do all of the family members fit into it?

I put the question to a cemetery caretaker who was polishing the brasswork on one of the tombs. His answer was something not found in New Orleans guidebooks.

When a family member (e.g., Aunt Beatrice) passes away the tomb is opened. Sitting just inside the entrance is the coffin of the last family member to be interred (e.g., Uncle Charlie who died three years ago). Uncle Charlie's remains are removed from his coffin, and the coffin is burned. Uncle Charlie is placed in a body bag and pushed further back in the vault on top of all of the other deceased family members, thus making room for Aunt Beatrice in her new coffin. This process can be carried on indefinitely. If you die in New Orleans, you certainly won't be lonely.

And, of course, sightseeing in New Orleans wouldn't be complete without a trip to the French Quarter, and specifically, Bourbon Street. To be certain that I witnessed

Bourbon Street in full regalia I went down there on Saturday night.

I should mention that public drinking seems to be perfectly legal and encouraged all over the city of New Orleans. In fact, if you light a cigarette in a crowded hotel elevator, you run the risk of blowing up the building. The drinkers really turn out on Bourbon Street on Saturday night. The street is blocked off from automobile traffic which is a good thing because your car would get corroded from spilled high-octane beverages being carried around by the weaving pedestrians.

Bourbon Street is a hodgepodge of frantic decadence. If it's like this on an ordinary night in June, I could only imagine what it must be like during Mardi Gras.

The street is lined with restaurants, bars, junky souvenir shops with X-rated T-shirts, and clubs with XXXX-rated floor shows. Girls were leaning over the wrought-iron railings on upper-story balconies and throwing beads and whimsical invitations to the crowd on the street below. They looked like college girls, but . . . well, maybe not. The quaint nineteenth-century buildings pulsed with two-hundred-decibel hard rock music(?) blaring from the open doors of the bars. I found only two places that featured New Orleans jazz. I muscled my way into one of them and found a table. There was some pretty fair Dixieland, but I didn't stay long. A glass of 7-UP cost over six dollars.

Far better Bourbon Street entertainment were the small African-American children with metal taps on their shoes, clicking out snappy rhythms on the sidewalks for tips from the passing tourists. (They seemed to do quite well, too.)

Police cars were stationed at the cross-street intersections, but they were apparently only interested in serious crimes, like muggings and murder, because they studiously ignored lesser offenses like public urination and intoxication, lewd conduct, and dope (people sharing a joint on the street is a common sight in New Orleans.)

I really do like New Orleans. I just think that the enchantment of the Big Easy after dark is overrated. Of course, I'm normally in bed by ten o'clock, so what do I know? But there are many enjoyable daylight-hour activities besides touring swamps and cemeteries. The stately old Southern homes lining St. Charles Avenue can be seen from an open-air streetcar, a real bargain at $1.25 per ride. You can have your palm read on Jackson Square as you shop for inexpensive original artwork done by artists who line the sidewalks. I enjoyed the mimes and street musicians on Royal Street. And of course, the town is filled with fabulous restaurants, although reservations are usually required. A fat wallet helps, although keep a tight grip on it when walking around..

I can heartily recommend a visit to New Orleans, but make it in January, not June. You won't have to take a shower every three hours.

APRIL IN PARIS

I n 1996 I'd already traveled to Europe three times, but had not visited Paris. Having only seen the Eiffel Tower, the Arc D' Triumph, and the Moulan Rouge in movies, it was about time to see these legendary sites in person.

At that time Karen and I had just begun traveling together. She thought that Paris would be a wonderful experience, so I had my Marquette travel agent book our flights, in April, of course. Everyone should experience April in Paris, right?

The travel agent also found economical accomodations in the Latin Quarter on the Left Bank. It just couldn't get any better.

The Left Bank has an interesting history involving famous people. Pablo Picasso, Henri Matisse, Jean-Paul Satre, Ernest Hemingway, and F. Scott Fitzgerald were just a few of the greats who hung out at Left Bank bistros while creating many of their greatest works.

The Latin Quarter is a Left Bank area, so named because in Medieval times Latin was widely spoken by students in the vicinity of the nearby University of Paris.

Our hotel was the Elysa-Luxembourg, and we immediately found out why it featured such reasonable rates. The word best describing the Elysa-Luxembourg is "small." Everything about it was small. Our taxi pulled up to the small hotel frontage. We checked in at the front desk in the very small lobby. The desk clerk directed us to the small elevator.

The inside dimensions of the elevator were four feet wide and three feet deep. Every closet I've ever used was larger than this elevator.

The desk clerk was apologetic. In broken English he explained, "I'm sorry but we don't have a bellman. You'll have to carry your own luggage because I have to remain at the desk. The rooms are on the fourth floor, and unfortunately you'll have to make two trips due to our small elevator."

He handed me the two room keys and carefully placed two of our suitcases into the elevator.

Karen gave the old tiny elevator a dirty look. "If you think that I'm getting into this stand-up coffin then you've got another think coming!" She clutched her purse and strode over to the stairway.

Our rooms were a tad larger than the elevator, but not by much. In each room a four-drawer dresser faced the foot of the double bed. However, the bottom two drawers couldn't be opened fully because the bed frame was in the way. To open the one tiny window in the room it was necessary to stand on the bed. The only place to put suitcases was on top of the dresser. A cozy setup. And the bath? Down the hall to the right.

After we had been staying at the Elysa-Luxembourg for a few days we noticed that Karen was the only woman guest in the hotel. It seemed that the Elysa-Luxembourg was well-known for catering to gay guys. The two of us were made more than welcome, though.

We soon encountered an unforeseen problem. Parisians enjoy late dinner. Latin Quarter restaurants didn't even open before 9:30 or 10PM, and this was entirely unacceptable for a couple of Upper Peninsula Finns who were used to having their dinner no later than 6PM.

But the problem was solved. We discovered a McDonald's restaurant nearby. Interestingly, at 6PM the place was always packed with, you guessed it, Parisians. Apparently many of them liked to eat at the same hour as normal people.

But Karen and I had ample opportunities to check out the local Parisian restaurants at lunchtime. As you might expect, the food was very good, and we also discovered a very interesting local custom. The French love their dogs, and their restaurants are no exception. You can walk into any dining establishment, including McDonalds, with your dog, and the wait staff will provide a place at your table for your furry best friend. That's right, your puppy will have a plate or bowl of his very own right on the table, and you both can enjoy your food together. The restaurants provide chairs of various heights for the dogs. (If you own a Great Dane no chair is necessary).

What did you say? You don't think this idea will go over too well in the U.S.? Well, in recent years Americans have begun to lavish more and more attention on their pets, and on a recent trip to Las Vegas we encountered countless small dogs on leads parading around in the Fashion Show Mall.

We tried to take in all of the famous Paris landmarks. We instructed our cabbie to drive slowly through the Arc D' Triumph. We hiked over to the Moulon Rouge, snapping photos along the way. At the Eiffel Tower I bought tickets for a ride to the top. At least that was the plan.

Karen is not crazy about heights and when the tower elevator stopped at a refreshment area half way up she was eager to get out, stating that this was as far up as she was going.

"But we've paid for tickets all the way to the top," I said.

"You go and I'll wait for you here."

We both got off at the halfway stop and I had a cup of French coffee while Karen stood close to the elevator hugging a post.

But we did something even more adventurous than riding up the Eiffel Tower. We took the French subway.

I don't remember where we wanted to go, but we walked down into a Left Bank subway station and approached the woman ticket seller sitting in a glass booth.

I explained in English where we wanted to go, and the woman looked irritated, mainly because I wasn't speaking French. Most countries around the world recognize English and try to cope with it, but not France. For them French is the only language worthy of speaking.

I had written our destination on a piece of paper and pointed to it. She whirled around and pointed at a multi-colored subway map on the booth wall. Speaking rapid

French she jabbed her finger at several points on the map, indicating, I thought, that we had to make at least one transfer along the way.

The ticket seller held out her hand, and I produced a fistful of French franc notes. She grabbed a couple and handed me two subway tickets and some coins in change. An electric buzzer opened the restraining bar and we stepped onto the subway platform.

I didn't have a clear idea of what to do, but I took an educated guess and we got onto the train that looked right to me and off we went.

I kept searching the platform signs every time we rolled into a station, but none of them matched any of the streets on my Paris map.

We finally got off and took the next train going back to where we came from. I was afraid that if we didn't cancel our plans there was a good chance we'd wind up in Switzerland.

Many Americans–like me–poke fun at the Parisians with their odd customs and intolerance of the English language, but there's definitely a unique and wonderful side of Paris. Parisians have an uncanny ability to preserve and beautify their past. The city is filled with 16th, 17th and 18th century buildings that are kept in magnificent condition. One morning Karen and I took an early walk along the Seine. It was just beautiful. The riverway was lined with spectacular ancient buildings and statues. It was like walking through a one-of-a-kind open-air museum.

Everyone should see Paris. You'll never experience anything like it. 🌍

ADVENTURES IN SCOTLAND

Karen and I had originally made arrangements to spend two weeks in Paris, but after seven days the cramped four walls of the Left Bank hotel room were beginning to close in on me. We'd also both had our fill of McBurgers for dinner every night, so we decided to move on.

I called my travel agent in Marquette who obligingly arranged a flight from Paris to Edinburgh, Scotland. We packed up our luggage and headed for Charles D'Gaulle Airport.

Scotland had always peaked my interest. It's not a big nation–275 miles long and 150 miles wide–about the size of Wisconsin. No one lives more than 40 miles from salt water.

The border between Scotland and England is just a line on the map, and the two countries have been joined constitutionally since 1707. But Scotland is very different from England, geographically and socially.

You'll hear Gaelic spoken, a language that defies interpretation. Tourists will discover lochs and glens where eagles soar. Lush meadows are filled with sheep and heather-covered moors are dotted with stone cottages, many with sod-covered roofs.

The people are very independent, but outsiders are welcome. In fact, we were about to discover that the people will do almost anything to please you. Tourist books tell visitors to remember one thing. Scotch is a whiskey and not the name of the proud people who live there. They're Scots. But they'll forgive you if you call them Scotch. Just don't call them English.

We landed at Edinburgh Airport, and a cab took us to a tree-lined street called Learmonth Gardens. I had told my travel agent that we wanted a Edinburgh hotel a bit more elegant than the sardine-can rooms in Paris, and she came through brilliantly.

The Channings Hotel is a grand old establishment consisting of several cleverly connected 19th century town homes, one of which being the former residence of Ernest Shackleton, the famous Antarctic explorer.

The rooms were large, high-ceilinged with a tall window overlooking the street, decorated with Victorian elegance, touched off with ornate four-poster beds.

My bathroom was fitted out with a white porcelain claw-foot tub, a sink with gold faucets, and a toilet with a highly varnished seat.

After using the toilet I twisted the fancy flush handle. Nothing happened. I tried it two or three more times with no result.

Mildly irritated, I walked into the bedroom and picked up the business end of the antique telephone next to the bed and dialed "O." A woman quickly came on the line.

"My toilet doesn't flush."

Within sixty seconds someone knocked on the door. A man in neatly pressed coveralls politely extended his hand.

I'm Jason, here to see about your toilet."

He strode into the bathroom and twisted the flush handle. It flushed perfectly.

"How did you do that?" I blurted out.

When the tank filled with water I twisted the handle. Nothing happened. I looked at Jason, figuring that he was pulling some kind of trick on me.

"Well, sir, perhaps it takes a bit of knackery, a particular flick of the wrist." He twisted the handle and the toilet flushed.

The toilet tank again filled with water, and Jason stepped aside, giving me words of encouragement. I turned the handle. It didn't flush.

By now Jason must have been thinking that I was some kind of spastic, lame-brained tourist, but he didn't twitch a whisker. "Well, sir, I believe I can do an adjustment or two and make it possible for you to use the device." He removed the top from the toilet tank and began tinkering with the adjustment on the arm.

About then another Channings maintenance man walked in, and the two of them began discussing the health of my toilet in a rapid brogue-laced conversation. More toilet parts were taken from the tank and scattered on the bathroom floor.

The maintenance supervisor soon appeared and began looking over the shoulders of his two men, offering technical advice when he thought necessary. By now the bathroom floor was filled with toilet parts.

Karen stuck her head in the bathroom door and wanted to know what was wrong with the toilet.

"Don't ask," I said.

The toilet was eventually put back together and I was given an intense lesson on using a Scottish flick of the wrist for toilet flushing. The problem was solved.

Karen and I had it in mind to do a quick driving tour of Scotland so the next day we took a cab to a car-rental agency in downtown Edinburgh. The car-rental people weren't at all bothered by the fact that I was an American who had never driven on the left-hand side of the road.

I filled out and signed the paperwork and was given the key to a small Renault.

Karen and I both paused and looked at the steering wheel on the right side. "Are you going to be able to drive this thing?" she asked cautiously.

"No problem," I replied.

I really hadn't given much thought to driving on the left side of the road until I climbed behind the steering wheel and put it to the test.

I no sooner had put the car into motion when Karen cried out, "You're too close over here!" It seemed that I was allowing too much clearance for oncoming traffic on my right side and getting over too close to parked cars on the left side.

Somehow we slowly and carefully made it back to Channings where I slowly and carefully parked the rental vehicle.

The next morning we started out at daybreak. Our plan was to drive over to Scotland's west coast, then turn north for awhile, then head over to the east coast where we'd visit the world-famous St. Andrews golf course and finally back to Edinburgh.

I slowly crept along the residential street, heading toward a east-west highway. Karen had resumed her "You're too close over here!" cry which didn't help my driving one bit.

But she was right. The Renault's left-side mirror clipped the right-side mirror of a parked car, knocking it neatly off onto the street.

I stopped the car and we got out and inspected the parked car. My first reaction was to quickly confess to the owner of the car and settle up for the damage. But who would that be? There was no name or address visible on the inside of the car. It was very early on Saturday morning and there was no one in sight.

"The only thing we can do is make a run for it," Karen solemnly stated.

Which is what we did. I scribbled a sincere note of apology and placed it along with the snapped-off mirror on the hood of the injured car and off we went. I always felt bad about that.

But our driving adventures had just begun. By mid afternoon we were nearing Scotland's west coast with Karen periodically reminding me, "You're too close over here!"

Suddenly I did indeed get more than too close to the left edge of the road. The left two wheels slid off the pavement. Unfortunately there was no shoulder on the roadway, and the wheels skidded down and hit the edge of a metal culvert that ran beneath the road.

After two violent "BANGS" I brought the Renault to a bumpy stop. We got out and took a look.

The two left tires were flattened. Even worse, both wheels were badly dented. The car was undriveable.

I knew we were only a few miles from a little town near the west coast. so we locked the Renault with our luggage inside and began walking. Worse yet, it was Easter Saturday and the few cars passing us were filled with family going to see grandma. Not one slowed down.

I was in a state of shock. We were on foot in a totally remote area of Scotland. Our belongings including clean underwear were in our broken rental car back up the road. On Easter weekend hotels and motels would probably be full. I had no idea if we would have a roof over our heads that night.

The one smart thing that I had done was to buy auto insurance on our rental car. When we finally reached a petrol station I called the toll-free number of the Royal Automobile Club, explaining our predicament. The woman who answered the phone didn't think it was any problem, and within the hour an auto-carrying truck pulled up. The teenage driver drove us to our disabled car.

The young driver deftly mounted our Renault on the back

of his truck. He told us that a nearby town close to where our Renault would be repaired would certainly have available rooms. We climbed into his truck and we took off.

Our driver was excited to meet people from the United States and wanted to impress us with his driving skills by providing a hair-raising ride up the snaky coastal road.

When we pulled up at a hotel I asked him, "Do you have any idea when the car will be fixed?"

The kid grinned, "Oh, I expect tomorrow sometime."

"But it's Easter Sunday."

"Not all of us will be in church."

Sure enough, the next morning we were having breakfast in the hotel dining room when we heard a horn honking. It was our young auto-carrier driver with our Renault on the back, now complete with two new wheels and tires. Would you get that kind of service on Easter Sunday in the United States? I think not.

We were on our way again, heading north. Later in the day we stopped at Loch Ness near the city of Inverness, hoping to catch a glimpse of the Loch Ness monster. It didn't happen. The monster was taking the holiday weekend off.

We turned east, then south, heading back toward Edinburgh. On the way was the city of St. Andrews, the birthplace of golf. Having taken up golf at age eleven, I had to see the world-famous St. Andrews golf course.

The Old Course at St. Andrews is the oldest and most famous golf course in the world. Interestingly, it's a public course. For the modest sum of 55 pounds you can reserve a tee time, although you most probably will have to wait for several months before your tee time comes up.

There's also a very private club at the St. Andrews course called the Royal and Ancient. I didn't know much of the history of the Royal and Ancient, but I knew that the clubhouse contained many artifacts belonging to legendary golfers like Walter Hagen, Ben Hogan, Bobby Jones, and others. I wanted to see these historic items.

Karen and I strode up to the Royal and Ancient clubhouse entrance where a uniformed man was standing at the door. It appeared that he was guarding the entrance.

"Sir, we'd like to go inside and look around. Is there an admission price?"

The guard's eyebrows shot up into his hairline. He sternly informed us that only the privileged members and their guests were allowed to enter the hallowed halls of the clubhouse. He could barely keep a straight face when he thought about my ridiculous request. I was to find out later that not even the Queen of England could enter the Royal and Ancient clubhouse unless she was a guest of a member.

Without any further incidents with the Renault we headed back to Edinburgh, and I dropped the car off at the rental agency. The accident didn't cost me a penny. God bless the Royal Automobile Club!

We sadly boarded a plane for home, both of us knowing that we'd be back. The charm of Scotland is the people. They will do anything to make your visit a pleasant one. Anything except let you enter the Royal and Ancient clubhouse. 🌍

DRIVING THROUGH DIXIE

When I was a kid I promised myself that I was going to visit every state in the Union. Back then there were only forty-eight, and it didn't seem like an overwhelming task.

But some years ago I realized that I was still six states shy, all in the southeast: Louisiana, Mississippi, Alabama, North and South Carolina, and Delaware. I decided to take a trip to hit them all.

Winter is a good time to explore the South (or anyplace else, for that matter) if you live in the U. P. I was reminded of this at the Marquette airport, watching a Mesaba Airlines employee snowblowing a path from the terminal door to the airplane so we could board. A first-rate blizzard was shaping up, but we managed to get off the ground without a hitch. I flew to Houston where I rented a car and began my journey through the South.

The first 150 miles were through east Texas. Texas is a big state, and Texans don't like to dawdle on the road because they've always got a long way to go. If you're only doing seventy-five, you'd best stay out of the fast lane and let folks pass you. In fact, on narrow two-lane roads truckers will charge up behind you and flash their lights, signaling you (I'm not making this up) to pull over on the shoulder to let them get by. Driving on the shoulder at seventy-five miles an hour is definitely dicey.

I spent the first afternoon driving through central Louisiana, listening to a country and western station. The DJ kept repeating that it was unseasonably cold. The local temperature was fifty-two degrees with a wind chill of thirty-six. He was talking about a *PLUS* thirty-six!

Louisiana–at least the part I saw–has lots of houses with sheet-metal roofs, and many are built on stilts. That's because the state is the mother of all swampland. If God ever decided to wring out Louisiana, the water level in the Gulf of Mexico would rise five hundred feet.

At sundown I arrived in Natchez, Mississippi, on the Mississippi River. Huge live oak and magnolia trees spread their long limbs across streets lined with restored antebellum mansions. I expected ladies in hoopskirts to come running out of the houses looking for Rhett Butler. A charming place.

One of my priorities on this trip was to get a good sampling of Southern cooking. In Natchez I had a seafood and okra gumbo dinner in a quaint riverside restaurant. Gumbo is very rich. A modest-size bowl has about the same caloric content as a Thanksgiving dinner. It's very tasty, but you won't need any more food for three or four days.

I spent much of the following day traveling on the Natchez Trace Parkway as far as Jackson, Mississippi. The parkway follows the path of an old trail used by nineteenth-century riverboat traders walking north on their return trip. It winds its way from Natchez to Nashville, Tennessee with nothing manmade on it except the two-lane road itself. No billboards or McDonalds. No trucks allowed (a pleasant change after Texas). A speed limit of fifty. Can you imagine such a place in the twenty-first century? I enjoyed every mile.

That evening in Meridian, Mississippi, I tried something called a "Naw'lins (New Orleans) Skillet" for dinner, a highly combustible mixture of rice, onions, peppers, shrimp, Cajun sausage, and plenty of spices. It's good, but if you dally too long over your dinner, the food eats its way through the plate. I quickly discovered that my dinner beverage of choice had to be water instead of wine because the water was necessary to put out the fire in my stomach.

The following day I drove through Alabama, passing through several burgs where *everyone* lived in mobile homes. Tornados regularly pull them apart, which is why there's always a big market for mobile homes in Alabama.

At a truck stop near Montgomery I tried to order some grits for lunch. The waitress said, "We don't serve grits. Can I get you some hash-browns?"

"I can get hash-browns in Michigan," I said.

But the next day I found grits in a restaurant in Newnan, Georgia. After all that, I found grits really aren't anything to write home about. It's white and pasty, kind of like Cream of

Wheat, which I never really liked. In fact, I think it *is* Cream of Wheat; the Southerners just wanted to call it something else. The grits were served with butter which didn't help much. Neither did adding pepper. I finally made it more tasty with catsup.

One thing I noticed, especially in Georgia, complete strangers will look at you and say, "How are you?" like they really mean it and want to know how you are. At first it was rather unsettling. I thought they were trying to sell me something. But no, they're just being friendly. It's a nice custom.

After three or four days it was still unseasonably cold down there, only getting into the low fifties during the day. I had occasion to tell people–hotel desk clerks, waiters, etc:–where I was from. As friendly as they were, a few of them accused me of bringing the Upper Michigan weather with me. It occurred to me that if it didn't warm up there pretty soon, things were going to get ugly.

I had plenty of occasions to ask for directions along the way, like: "How far is it to Wilmington, North Carolina?" I discovered that women won't tell you how many miles it is, because mileage isn't important to them. They say, "Wilmington? Oh, that's an hour from here."

Men always tell you in miles, straight out. That works for me.

I especially enjoyed Savannah, Georgia's oldest and most charming city. At the time of the Revolutionary War, Savannah was a large bustling seaport, but today the impression is vastly different. Savannah hasn't caught the hurry-scurry disease afflicting most modern-day cities. Everyone in Savannah moves at a leisurely pace. There's plenty of parking on the wide tree-shaded streets if you have a notion to pull over and people-watch from one of the benches in the many pocket-size parks that dot the historic downtown area.

Yet Charleston, South Carolina, one-hundred miles up the Atlantic coast, was an entirely different story. After checking into a hotel on the outskirts of town, I acted on the advice of the desk clerk and drove into downtown Charleston to have dinner at Hyman's, reportedly the home of the best seafood in South Carolina.

I carefully hugged the slow lane to stay clear of the crazies racing up and down the narrow streets. I thought maybe these bat-out-of-hell motorists were transplanted Southern Californians, but they might just have been locals practicing for the next hurricane evacuation.

I finally found the restaurant, but there was no–and I mean absolutely *NO*–available parking spaces for blocks around. I settled for dinner at a Ruby Tuesday restaurant near my hotel. In 1861 the first shot of the Civil War was fired at Charleston. I think they were squabbling over a parking space.

Charleston's Patriots Point Naval Museum was a more enjoyable experience. Patriots Point, in the Charleston harbor, is the home of a collection of World War II naval vessels, including the aircraft carrier *Yorktown*. Being a longtime

WW-II buff, I paid the admission and eagerly boarded the carrier. This ship, nicknamed "The Fighting Lady," saw considerable action in the South Pacific. It sustained severe damage when several Kamikaze planes hit it during the invasion of Okinawa in the final days of the war. Later in its distinguished career, the ship recovered the crew of *Apollo 8*, the first manned spacecraft to orbit the moon. The hanger bay housed several WW-II navy planes which I knew intimately from my preadolescent model-building days. I climbed all over the *Yorktown*, an arduous task since the carrier is at least ten stories tall from keel to superstructure, and there are no elevators.

Equally interesting was the submarine *Clamagore*. Talk about cramped quarters! The torpedo crew had to bunk right next to the torpedoes; they really took their work home with them.

World War II submarines couldn't stay submerged very long, about fifteen hours max. After that, the air got so foul that your cigarette wouldn't stay lit. That's right, they were allowed to smoke inside this tin fish, and *under water* to boot.

From Charleston I pressed on up the Atlantic coast. It warmed up to 70 degrees as I proceeded north, a good thing because that stopped people from bugging me about bringing our U.P. weather to the South.

The Carolinas are golf havens, and Myrtle Beach, South Carolina, is the golf capital of the nation. It's right on the Atlantic, except that you can't see the ocean for the solid wall of condominiums bought up by the tens of thousands of retired golfers from the Midwest.

I proceeded east toward the Outer Banks of North Carolina. Eastern North Carolina is really desolate country. There are "Watch for Bears" signs, and they're not kidding. I saw a dead-bear roadkill on the shoulder of the road, something you don't often come across.

The Wright Brothers Memorial at Kill Devil Hills, North Carolina, on the Outer Banks was one of the highlights of the trip. It brought a lump in my throat to stand at the spot where the brothers made that historic flight in 1903–albeit only 120 feet, less than the length of a Boeing 747.

I crossed the Chesapeake Bay and proceeded north. Only one state left on my list now. Delaware. I clipped the southwest corner of it on my way to Baltimore where I was catching a plane to Detroit the next morning. What I saw of Delaware wasn't very exciting, kind of like the southern portion of lower Michigan, but I didn't really give the poor little state a fair shake. Someday I have to go back and take a better look at it.

It was business as usual when I returned to the U.P.; the snow was still falling. I picked up my suitcase from the airport luggage carousel and stoically dug out my long-forgotten mitts and muffler.

HUNTING THE ELUSIVE MOOSE

I've always had this irrational affinity for cold, lonesome, remote northern places where few people live and nobody in their right mind would ever want to visit in the winter. I suppose that's why I'm living in the U.P., and also why I've always wanted to visit Newfoundland. I fulfilled my wish when Karen and I took a trip there.

We flew into St. Johns, the provincial capital of Newfoundland. St Johns is the oldest port city on the North American continent, originally settled in the early 1600's. About the size of Green Bay, it's a charming mini-San Francisco with steep streets filled with brightly painted Victorian row houses.

The people are very friendly. In St. Johns if you're even *thinking* about stepping off the curb to cross the street, drivers a half block up the street will slam on the brakes and wait for you. Definitely not like large U.S. cities where motorists frequently drive up onto the sidewalk trying to run you down.

Newfoundland, the easternmost province of Canada,

is a lonely island jutting far out into the North Atlantic. So far out, in fact, that during World War II prowling German U-boats often fired torpedoes into the harbor of St. Johns to disrupt wartime shipping. The local population (Newfies) fondly refer to their lonesome island home as "The Rock." It's a big rock, though, larger than Lower Michigan. If you drive from St Johns, on the craggy, windswept east coast, to Corner Brook, a town on the west coast, it's the same distance as from Marquette to Chicago.

Newfies are individualists, complete with their own unique time zone. When it's nine o'clock in New York City, it's ten-thirty in Newfoundland. The locals brag that if the world is going to end at midnight it'll already be one-thirty in Newfoundland. I kept asking the people how Newfoundland happened to have this funny time zone one half hour off from everyone else. No one seemed to know, but the expressions on their faces said, "Why not?"

The inhabitants must have been sampling a lot of rum back in the days when they were naming their towns. There are burgs called Blow Me Down, Cow Head, Deadman's Bay, Leading Tickles, Goobies, Little Seldom, and Joe Batt's Arm (it sounds like the arm wasn't attached to Joe Batt when the town was named). We drove through a trio of sleepy little hamlets named Heart's Content, Heart's Desire, and Heart's Delight.

After a few days our trip assumed a pressing mission. It was all the moose's fault. Every time we were preparing to get on the road to journey to another Newfoundland town, people would advise us to "Watch out for moose!" It seems that Newfoundland is overrun with moose. They create a nuisance by wandering into towns or stepping out in front of unsuspecting motorists. Moose-caution signs were everywhere on the roadways. We became convinced that there would be lengthy delays while large herds of moose ambled across the road directly in front of our car.

This immediately piqued Karen's interest because she'd never seen a moose, and she's a real animal lover. When she was married and living in Texas she had four dogs, a cat, and supported several assorted wild critters and birds that regularly fed from food dishes left out for them. She befriended a rat. Not a white laboratory rat, mind you, but your plain old garden-variety ordinary gray rat. One night Karen's cat chased a rat to the edge of their swimming pool, and the rat jumped into the water to escape. Karen found the rat the next morning, exhausted, swimming out his final moments in the center of the pool. Her husband, Ron, scooped it out with a long-handled net and mercifully put it over the fence, hoping that it would dash to freedom. But the rat, realizing that it owed its life to Ron and Karen, hung around, skulking around the edge of the property, occasionally frolicking with the dogs in their exercise yard, always hoping in some humble rat-like way to repay the kindness.

Karen decided she just *had* to spot a moose. As we traveled from one town to another she had her camera on the car seat, loaded and ready to fire. We peered intently into forests, swamps, and meadowlands. We glanced up side streets of the many small villages. At lunchtime we carefully watched the highway through restaurant windows to see if a moose would jump out in front of the passing cars. No moose.

"The moose is a mythical beast," Karen finally muttered.

I shook my head. "I saw one outside of Michigamme just last year, driving back from the Copper Country."

"I don't believe it," she snapped. "You had too much dinner wine in Houghton."

"No. They really exist. Just yesterday you bought postcards with pictures of moose."

"Trick photography!"

On our last night in St. Johns we went to a restaurant that featured all manner of wild game dishes on the menu.

The waiter seated us, handed us our menus, and smiled pleasantly. "We have everything on the menu except the moose. I'm afraid it's not available at this time."

"That figures," Karen said dryly.

The trip drew to an otherwise pleasant conclusion, but we didn't see a single moose. Karen did however get a nice picture of a Newfoundland goat. She can provide copies for anyone who's interested.

COME WIZ ME TO ZA CASBAH

I n 1938 Charles Boyer and Hedy Lamarr starred in a movie titled *Algiers*. Younger generations may not have heard of Boyer and Lamarr, but in their day they were Hollywood's Brad Pitt and Angelina Jolie.

In the movie Boyer plays Pepe le Moko, a master criminal forced to remain in the sanctuary of the menacing Casbah quarter of Algiers, where policemen dared not enter. Pepe holds court in his domain, surrounded by various unsavory characters, and his existence, although drab, is at least tolerable...until a beautiful woman (Hedy Lamarr) comes to the Casbah on a thrill-seeking visit. The two are fascinated by each other and enter into a clandestine, short-lived affair. But Pepe cannot remain apart from her and eventually leaves the Casbah in search of his love, forfeiting his safety with tragic results.

Algiers, the movie, achieved a quirky immortality when Boyer, with his dark, liquid eyes, gazed at Hedy Lamarr and in a masterfully seductive French accent uttered the now-famous line:

"Come wiz me to za Casbah."

So why I am I telling you all this? Because I just returned from the Casbah. Karen I were on a November cruise in the western Mediterranean, stopping at ports on the Spanish coast, Gibraltar, and North Africa. We didn't visit the Algiers Casbah but instead the Casbah in Tangier, Morocco, not far from Algiers. Many cities in North Africa have Casbah districts, which are really ancient fortresses with equally ancient communities within. All are exotic, intriguing, and more than a little frightening. An outsider has no business wandering around in any of them after the sun goes down.

The city of Tangier has a wicked reputation in its own right. When the cruise ship docked we boarded a tour bus to see the city, wisely deciding that a place renowned for international spies, dope dealers, flim-flam artists, and pickpockets was best explored in the safety of a large group under the wing of an English-speaking guide.

After stopping at several preliminary points of interest, the bus pulled up outside a towering old wall made of huge gray stones. Inside was the Casbah district of Tangier. We disembarked and obediently trooped close behind our tour guide through a large gate in the old wall.

Everything you might have heard or read about a Casbah is absolutely true. Mysterious looking people were bustling about in all directions, bumping into us without a word of apology. Sinister-looking men stared at us from doorways. There were no police in sight. No taxis. Not even a McDonald's. My wallet was securely stored in a zippered vest pocket, but I had a death grip on the outside of the pocket nonetheless.

Picture a plate of spaghetti, each piece coated with cobblestones, and you have the Casbah street system, a torturous maze of twisting, very narrow alleyways with no logical layout whatsoever. The buildings date back to who-knows-what century. There are no street signs, but nothing really qualifies as a street anyway.

We soon discovered that the Tangier Casbah is home to the world's greatest hustlers. Dark-skinned peddlers thrust fistfuls of Rolex (you bet they are) watches, miniature brass camels, and handmade copper bracelets in our faces, crying out prices in broken English. I tried to ignore them, concentrating on following the guide, but Karen loves to interact with salespeople and began talking to the sellers. Smelling a likely prospect for a sale, they descended on her like a plague of locusts. She quickly wound up buying several copper bracelets.

"What did you pay for them?" I asked, inspecting the bracelets as we scurried along after our guide.

"Two dollars apiece," she announced smugly, proud of her purchases.

The bracelets weren't at all bad looking, and I decided I wanted some too.

"One dollar apiece," I said to the next bracelet peddler.

"One dollar?" he howled in anguish. "I lose money!"

I shrugged and kept on moving through the mass of people.

The peddler trotted after me, holding out the bracelets. "Okay, okay, one dollar," he relented. "How many you want?"

I bought several. In fact, moments later, intoxicated with my new-found bargaining skill, I purchased a five-inch-high brass camel for five dollars.

A favorite ploy of any Casbah guide is to get a group of tourists hopelessly lost in the tangle of streets and then herd them into his brother-in-law's store where they become a captive audience for a sales pitch. We were ushered up a narrow stairway in such a shop and seated on wooden benches in a large room, whereupon the proprietor–no doubt a close relative of our guide–had his numerous sons drag out a vast, colorful array of handmade carpets from the back and unfurl them, one after another, at our feet. As each carpet was plopped onto the growing pile, the store owner bragged on it at great length. He droned on for a half hour until I finally got up and went downstairs where there was a good assortment of other merchandise.

I was poking around in a bin of brass candlesticks when another store manager, dressed in a flowing, dark galabeeyah (robe) discreetly tapped me on the shoulder and pointed to a woman from our cruise ship who had followed me downstairs.

"Is that your wife?" he inquired discretely.

I shook my head.

"Too bad," he murmured with a trace of a smile. He held up a fancy Moroccan cane with an elegantly embossed silver head. "I would have offered you two of these in trade for her."

I course I knew he was joking...at least I *thought* he was joking. I laughed heartily, but not wanting to press the negotiations any further, I went back upstairs. The carpet commercial was still raging, so I sat down next to Karen who was fast slipping into a deep funk from the marathon sales pitch.

Suddenly the manager from downstairs again appeared at my side, whispering in my ear as he pointed at Karen. "*This one must be your wife, eh? I think I would go three canes for her.*"

"I'll tell her," I replied. "She'll be pleased to know that."

We survived the Casbah, but only after Karen purchased a pair of sterling silver salt and pepper shakers and I bought a leather jacket. Apparently satisfied with this ransom, the guide took us safely back to the ship.

All I have to do now is figure out what to do with this brass camel. Anyone interested? I'll give you a good price . . . ten dollars. Okay, okay, I'll take five. No lower, though, I lose money otherwise.

CRUISING 101

Karen and I both love to travel on the big ships, and we heartily recommend it for a vacation experience.

But for the benefit of people thinking of embarking on their first cruise, before you put your money down let me give you an introductory course in cruising. Call it Cruising 101.

Cruising is the ultimate in high-on-the-hog travel. No battling your way up to the car-rental counter at the airport or struggling with unwieldy road maps as you inch along through congested traffic on the interstates. No wrestling your luggage in and out of hotels. With cruising you simply stroll up the gangway onto this enormous, fourteen-story, gleaming white ship where you're greeted by a crewperson so friendly that he has to restrain himself to keep from hugging you. You're escorted to your stateroom where your baggage will be promptly delivered, and you'll be left in the hands of a smiling room steward. The steward points out all of the amenities of the stateroom, stating (every other word he utters is "sir") that if there's any little thing you need just call him on the phone next to your bed. After that you unpack, lay back and relax and look forward to waking up in a different country every morning.

The steward is personally assigned to your stateroom for the duration of the cruise, and you quickly find that while you're elsewhere on the ship he sneaks in and makes your bed, vacuums, cleans the bathroom, replenishes the ice cubes and tidies up all of the little souvenir knickknacks that you bought in the last port of call.

In the evening while you're at dinner in the dining room he comes into your stateroom again, cleans it up, then places a mint on your pillow, fashions a cute puppy dog or monkey out of one of your bath towels and places it on your bed.

All of your food is included in the cruise fare, and believe me, food is not in short supply. For four hours breakfast is served in at least three different locations throughout the ship. And if that isn't enough, the hamburger and hot-dog cafe opens at midmorning to tide over any passengers feeling faint from hunger. This goes on all day long. At dinner you have your choice of a half dozen lavishly presented entrees with all the trimmings. Steak, lobster, short ribs, shrimp and much more. Plus, the dessert selections are endless. Food presentation winds up with a pizza station open well past midnight. And of course there's 24-hour room service for the truly desperate eaters.

Many people religiously participate in each and every one of these eating events. Cruise ships generally sit lower in the water at the end of the voyage due to the increased tonnage of the passengers.

Nightly floor shows with live orchestras, singers, scantily clad show girls, magicians, and comedians are included at no cost. As are first-run movies, lectures, and classes on everything from line dancing to napkin folding (I've tried both, and line dancing is easier).

Lastly, while all this is going on you get transported on this large gleaming white ship to exotic ports of call where you can disembark and hobnob with the friendly local inhabitants.

How much does this cost? Well, maybe you've responded to an ad advertising something like:

SEVEN DAY CARIBBEAN HOLIDAY
Visit romantic Cancun, Cozumel, Belize and Honduras.
ONLY $649!

Do the math. Only $92 a day! You get all of the above mentioned for the price of a moderately priced hotel room.

Can the cruise industry actually make money charging people $92 a day? The answer; of course not! Here's what happens:

Cruise lines have a lot of expenses to meet. The fuel mileage on one of those floating cities is about one foot to the gallon. They have to pay, house, and feed a crew of hundreds of people and maintain the ship in tiptop condition.

How do they pay for all this? It starts even before you board the ship. You've just been processed through registration and security in the pier terminal and heading toward the ship's gangway when a friendly crew person asks you to stand in front of this large color photograph of the ship and smile. A ship's photographer snaps your picture. The photo later appears on a photo-gallery wall in the ship, along with those of every other passenger on board. Your picture generally looks pretty good because you're happy to be embarking on such a wonderful, inexpensive vacation. But if you want the picture, and most people do, it'll cost you fifteen dollars for one 5X7 print.

And they're not done with the cameras yet. You're sitting in the ship's large dining room, happily forking down chunks of filet, when an evil-looking Caribbean pirate comes up behind you and places a wooden cutlass across your Adam's apple. Everyone at the table laughs, and the pirate's mate snaps your picture. This will also appear on the gallery wall the next morning, for sale, of course. Or you're leaving the dining room when an extremely curvaceous show girl in net stockings up to her armpits comes up, takes your arm, and gives you a dazzling smile. A flash goes off. Who could resist buying a copy of that picture to show the boys back home?

Another method of extracting money from the passengers is selling water. Before your dining-room waiter takes your order he'll hold up bottled water imported from France. "Would you be interested in bottled water or just have (dramatic pause here) the *ship's water*?" The ominous tone of those last two words implies that the ship's water is pumped up from the bilge through rusty pipes. Something you wouldn't even want to wash your dog with, much less drink. Of course, most people order the bottled water which, by the way, costs about five dollars a bottle.

At times the seas will get choppy. If you began to feel a bit queasy, the ship's drugstore sells seasick tablets. Six dollars for eight tablets. There are other handy items sold in the drugstore. You can buy a roll of breath mints–normal price, forty cents–for four dollars. One of those little Kodak throwaway cameras–Wal-Mart price $4.40–costs $19.95 on board ship.

There's a beauty salon on board. A man's haircut costs $45. Don't even ask what they charge the women.

Every cruise ship now has what they call an Internet Cafe, with terminals where you can email your friends, telling them what a wonderful time you're having. Keep it brief, though, because you're charged mightily.

Coffee, tea, and milk are served free of charge in the dining room, but if you wish to have soft drinks, wine or cocktails with your meal that's another story. You'd better look over the wine list before you make a selection because if you let the sommelier select a bottle of pinot noir it might cost half the price that you paid for the cruise.

On a cruise ship no one really notices these charges because there's no money changing hands. Your magnetic cruise card is your on-board credit card. You can purchase anything from photos, breath mints, French water, liquor, massages, haircuts, cameras, clothing, jewelry, pieces of art, emails and telephone calls. You don't notice the fantastically inflated prices because you're not reaching for your wallet.

Oh, and I should mention: every cruise ship has a casino. Merely give the casino cashier your cruise card, and she'll give you as many chips as you want.

If you send your undies off to the ship's laundry you'll be charged about $25 for a modest-size bag.

On the final morning, hours before you're to disembark the ship, someone slips an envelope under your stateroom door. It contains a neat, itemized list of everything you charged on your cruise card during the journey. And for your added convenience, so you won't have to trouble yourself trying to figure out how much to tip the cabin stewart and dining-room waiters, an "automatic gratuity" has been added to your bill. The total amount of the bill will usually make the original come-on price of $649 look like chump change.

If you open your stateroom door at that hour, you'll swear you're on the sinking Titanic for all of the screaming going on.

But does cruising have to cost a ton of money? No. The free ship's water is just as pure as the French bottled water. Bring along your camera and take your own pictures. Have your hair done before you board the ship. At dinner look at the wine list and order the cheapest bottle. Bring your own seasick medication. Bypass the casino.

Okay, so buy a tee shirt with a picture of the cruise ship on it. It won't break the bank.

OUR BIRMINGHAM BUDDIES

Some years ago Karen and I were cruising the Caribbean, and one morning at breakfast in the ship's dining room we happened to be sitting across the aisle from another couple. The gentleman peaked my interest because he bore an uncanny resemblance to a character actor I'd seen in many British movies. This actor had made a career portraying all manner of evil and deranged villains.

The man sitting across from us was bald, had penetrating eyes behind framed spectacles, and was conversing with his wife in a British accent. The accent completed the close match to the actor's persona.

As Karen and I got up to leave, I leaned over to the man and said, "Has anyone ever told you that you look just like Donald Pleasance?"

That was the beginning of a long, happy and sometimes wacky friendship.

Jean and Ian Fawcett are retired and live quietly in Birmingham, England. However, quietly is not a word that best describes Ian Fawcett. Silence is not his strong suit. If you sit down with Ian and begin a discussion–any subject– he'll immediately tell you everything you should know about the issue.

This is not an unusual trait with many people who aren't as smart as they think they are. But interestingly, I've found that Ian's quite the opposite. He's extremely bright and well read. My problem is understanding what he's saying. Ian has a pronounced British accent and talks at the speed of a tobacco auctioneer. At times when he takes a breath, I'll turn to his wife, Jean, and ask, "What did he just say?" She'll translate Ian at a slower pace.

To make matters worse, Ian is a big fan of using rhyming slang. Never heard of it, you say? Neither had I until we met Ian.

Rhyming slang is a quirky British way of speaking where a common word is replaced with a cute rhyming phrase of two or three words. The word "stairs" would become "apples and pears." "Wife" would be "trouble and strife." "Phone" would be "dog and bone." "Eyes" would be "mince pies." "Feet" would be "plates of meat." "Wig" would become "Syrup of figs." Pretty cute, huh?"

Rhyming slang dates back to the mid 19th century, most likely originating in London. Some researchers believe that marketplace traders began using it among themselves to discuss transaction tactics while potential customers were within earshot. Another theory is that criminals used it to communicate with one another to confuse the police.

Then some brainy Brit (probably in a pub after six pints) thought that the conversation could be sped up by eliminating the secondary rhyming word. So "apples and pears" would become just "apples."

Consider an ordinary sentence like:

"It nearly knocked me off my feet. He was wearing a wig! I ran up the stairs and got on the phone with my wife and said 'I couldn't believe my eyes!'"

Now if two Englishmen are in a pub speaking in rhyming slang this conversation would be as follows:

"It nearly knocked me off me plates. He was wearing a syrup! I ran up the apples and got on the dog to my trouble and said, 'I couldn't believe my mincers'"

I am not making this up! Conversations like this actually go on in England.

Americans think that this nutty way of speaking would never be used in the United States. However, some examples of rhyming slang have crept into our own usage of the English language. We often refer to money as "bread." It actually came from the British rhyming slang phrase "bread and honey" for money.

Karen and I have been on many cruises with the Fawcetts, and when we're sitting down at dinner in the ship's dining room, after a few cocktails Ian might lapse into rhyming slang. The wait staff passing our table will stop and give him a double take. I just smile and nod.

Jean and Ian have become close friends over the years. Jean has been battling serious medical problems for some time, so we've been trying to schedule our vacations to accommodate her health restrictions. We're making it happen, and Karen and I hope to enjoy many more cruises with these two dear friends.

Who knows? Some day I even may even figure out what Ian is saying.

A CRUISING PROBLEM

I n recent years several cruise ships have experienced a series of mishaps. Who can forget the jarring sight of the 114,000 ton megaship, the *Costa Concordia,* lying on its side in shallow water off the Italian coast. A navigation error brought the Concordia too close to shore, capsizing the large vessel. Thirty-two passengers were lost.

February, 2013: An engine-room fire left the *Carnival Triumph* without power in the middle of the Gulf of Mexico. Three tug boats pulled the ship into the port of Mobile, Alabama. During the towing operation the Triumph operated under emergency power, limiting air conditioning to public areas. Thousands of electric toilets malfunctioned, resulting in massive overflows of sewage throughout the ship.

Again in February, 2013 the *Costa Allegra* lost all power when a fire broke out in the electric generator room. It took tug boats two days to tow the ship back into port to allow the passengers to disembark. Costa took the ship out of service, and it will be either sold or scrapped.

March, 2013: Another mammoth cruise ship, the *Carnival Dream,* experienced mechanical problems while in the Caribbean port of St. Maartens. After many frustrating days it was finally determined that the problem couldn't be easily fixed, and all passengers had to be flown home.

And these are just a few examples. Many other shipboard mechanical, electrical and crew-error problems have put cruisers in harms way and inconvenienced thousands of passengers.

But Karen and I are veteran cruisers and situations like these haven't deterred us from getting aboard another ship. After all, problems encountered while cruising only happen to other people, right?

Well, not exactly. Let me tell you a true story.

In April, 2012 Karen and I flew to Fort Lauderdale, Forida and boarded the *Ruby Princess* for a transatlantic cruise to Europe. The *Ruby Princess* is an elegant 113,000 ton ship, 16 decks high, eight restaurants, an unknown number of cocktail lounges, spa/beauty parlor, art gallery, gambling casino, miniature golf course, and a fine assortment of boutiques. The Ruby is a floating city.

After a smooth six days crossing the Atlantic, our first stop was Madeira, an island in the eastern Atlantic.

In 1419 Madeira was discovered by Portuguese seamen during a storm. The following year a Portuguese expedition landed on the island and took possession on behalf of the Portuguese crown. Settlers cleared forest land and began raising wheat and sugar cane. At this point they also began developing the now-famous Madeira wine which is currently being exported all over the world.

The island of Madeira is now considered a sub-tropical vacation paradise and during the winter months attracts thousands of Europeans fleeing cold weather.

The *Ruby Princess* docked at Funchal, the major city on the island. Karen and I disembarked to go into the city for some picture-taking, and I intended to sample the famous Madeira wine.

We were walking toward a dockside shuttle bus bound for the city center when a sneaky curb reached up and grabbed my shoe. I tripped and fell, making a hard one-point landing on my right buttock.

One of the ship's staff helped me up and asked if I was okay. I couldn't feel any sharp pain in my lower region, so I nodded and thanked him, and Karen and I boarded the shuttle bus.

In the center of Funchal we stopped at a sidewalk café where I had a glass of Madeira wine. We then proceeded on foot down a tree-lined street so Karen could take pictures of the local architecture.

Suddenly my backside began feeling stiff. I reached back and rubbed my rear pocket. I couldn't see it but there was a huge swelling on my buttock.

"Karen! Take a look at my butt!"

She thought I was just acting silly and paid no attention, continuing to snap pictures.

In a matter of minutes my right leg stiffened up so badly

that I could no longer walk. By now Karen realized that something was very wrong. She hailed a taxi, and she and the driver slowly and carefully inserted me into the rear seat. We returned to the *Ruby Princess*. The ship's staff provided a wheelchair, rolled me up the gangway and into the ship's hospital.

A ship's doctor told me to drop my trousers and undershorts so he could take a look.

His eyes widened. "My gosh, I've never seen anything like that!"

This is definitely not something you want to hear from an examining doctor. A wall mirror allowed me to get my first glimpse of the damage from the fall. There was a huge purple lump emerging from my right buttock. I was giving birth to a giant plum.

The doctor delicately probed it. "I think there's a good possibility you have something torn or broken in there. You need to get an X-ray."

I nodded. "Well, let's do it."

"We don't have an X-ray machine on the ship. We'll have to take you to a hospital in Funchal."

A ship with over 3000 passengers–mostly old fogeys for whom falling is a way of life–doesn't have an X-ray machine? I couldn't believe it.

I said to the doctor, "But the ship is scheduled to sail in less than a hour and a half. If I have to be taken into the city for an X-ray, isn't that cutting it close?"

The doctor kept staring at my lump. "Well, if the X-ray

finds something broken or torn then a medical procedure may be necessary at the local hospital."

It took a moment for that to register. "You mean....the ship would leave without me?"

He nodded, "It's possible. Cruise ships have to stick to a tight schedule. I'll order an ambulance to take you to a local hospital, and a few of the ship's staff will help your companion pack up your belongings in the stateroom. Don 't worry, we'll have you safely at the hospital and your luggage will be off the ship before we have to sail."

Don't worry? Don't worry? I'm about to be dropped off on a small non-English-speaking island much closer to Africa than the U.S., not to mention that I can't walk, and he tells me not to worry?

The next 20 minutes were chaotic. Karen and I had a quick, urgent conference concerning what she had to do if I was forced to stay in the hospital in Funchal. I gave her my wallet in the event that she had to make a fast financial settlement at the purser's desk. Two of the ship's staff immediately escorted her up to our suite to pack up our belongings.

"The ambulance is here on the dock," the doctor announced. "They'll get you to the hospital." He quickly wrote up a report to be presented to the medical staff at the Funchal hospital. Two members of the crew placed me in a wheelchair and prepared to wheel me out of the ships hospital.

"Wait a minute," I yelled. "Karen's coming with me!"

The doctor said, "It may be a while before your luggage gets down to the gangway, and we can't keep the ambulance waiting. You'll have to leave now."

One of the men began wheeling me out.

"What hospital am I going to? Karen's got to know!"

"I don't know," the ship's doctor replied. "It's Sunday and most of them will be closed to new patients. One of them should be able to take you, though."

I frantically tried to get out of the wheelchair but I couldn't stand up. One of the attendants grabbed the wheelchair handles and wheeled me down the gangway to the waiting ambulance. Two Funchal ambulance attendants carefully placed me on the gurney in the rear of the vehicle, and we took off into the city.

One attendant rode in back, sitting next to my gurney. He kept glancing at me and nodding and smiling. I smiled back. The guy finally elected to practice his severely limited English on me, but he didn't give me words of comfort. He wanted to discuss the local economy.

"Madeira ees broke!" he announced loudly. "No money!" He then put his hands out, palms up, forming a bowl. "We go to Germany, an' say, 'We need money.' But no money from Germany!" He threw up his hands in frustration. "We broke! We broke!"

I nodded in sympathy, but my mind was elsewhere. A chilling realization was creeping into my bones. The only thing I had on my person was my passport. Karen had my wallet with my money and credit cards. She had no idea which hospital I was being taken to because the *Ruby Princess* staff didn't know either. I wasn't even sure if Karen was going to be able to get off the ship before it sailed. Some non-English-speaking doctor was going to examine me and probably perform a who-knows-what procedure on my body, and I wasn't even going to be able to pay for it.

We pulled up at a nondescript building. There was no sign on it. It could have been a hospital, a funeral home or the back end of the local Walmart.

Apparently it was a hospital because the ambulance attendants lifted my gurney out onto the sidewalk and placed me in a wheelchair. A white-coated nurse wheeled me up the ramp to the entrance. She nodded and smiled. I smiled back. I was wheeled into an examining room. The nurse left and closed the door.

I stared around the room. There were boldly-lettered signs on the wall which appeared to be cautionary messages for the benefit of patients, but they were written in what I assumed was Portuguese so the information was lost on me.

My butt and right leg were now aching furiously, and there was no question that I wasn't going anywhere without a lot of help.

I looked at my watch. The *Ruby Princess* was scheduled to sail in twenty minutes, and I hadn't even seen a doctor yet. I was about to be marooned on a foreign island off the coast of Africa. Would I have to learn Portuguese so I could work in the hospital kitchen to pay off my medical bill?

The door opened and a white-coated gentleman entered.

He stuck out his hand. "Good afternoon. I'm Dr. Gomes."

HE SPEAKS ENGLISH! I would have gotten up and hugged him if I could have gotten up. I enthusiastically shook his hand and introduced myself.

"Let's see what you have." The doctor helped me stand up, and I dropped my trousers and undershorts.

Dr. Gomes briefly glanced at my right buttock. "A gluteal hematoma. We'll X-Ray it, but I don't think we'll find any real damage."

The doctor and a nurse promptly got me on a gurney and took me to the X-Ray room. A technician snapped a few pictures of my lower region.

Moments later Dr. Gomes looked at the X-Ray film. "Nothing broken or torn. You must put ice on it several times a day to reduce the swelling. I'll prescribe an anti-inflammatory and pain medication that the ship's hospital will be able to provide.

"You mean...I can still make it back to the ship? It hasn't sailed yet?"

Dr. Gomes grinned. "We deal with cruise-ship passengers all the time. Trust me, you'll make it."

I was breathing huge sighs of relief while being wheeled down the hallway. Feeling more social now, I asked the doctor, "You've been to the United States?"

He shook his head. "Never have." Then he proudly added, "I've twice been to London, though." He wanted it known that he wasn't just some small-town doctor.

I was wheeled to the admissions area at the front

entrance. Karen was waiting for me. We were never so glad to see each other. The woman has a very practical mind set, and before she hugged me she handed me my wallet.

Accompanying her was a local young man who was employed by Princess Cruise Lines to assist passengers needing emergency transportation while in Funchal. He had brought Karen from the ship to the hospital and was going to take the two of us back to the ship.

I took out a credit card and paid the hospital bill. It was over $600, but worth every penny. I was being set free.

In the coming days, after sitting on countless ice packs, the swelling went down and I was able to walk and enjoy the rest of the cruise.

Now, if you're a person of a certain age and thinking of taking a cruise, don't worry about the food or accommodations. They'll be fine. Just find out if the ship has an X-ray machine.

A CARIBBEAN CHRISTMAS

One year Karen, her two daughters, Kara and Lisa, and I went on a Christmas cruise to the Western Caribbean–a truly terrible place where you have to endure constant sunshine and wind-chill factors of 75 degrees above zero.

To guard against "Cruise Flu," a contagious virus that's been known to circulate among cruise ships, I took along plenty of Pepto Bismol, aspirin, and hand sanitizer and avoided shaking hands with everyone during the entire voyage. As a final precaution I stayed away from drinking water, wisely limiting my fluid intake to wine and beer. I believe that this last safeguard was the most effective virus deterrent since I felt really swell throughout the cruise.

Vacationing on a cruise ship isn't just lounging around in a deck chair soaking up the sun. No indeed. To ensure that there was precious little time to rest and relax, the ship's crew had plenty of jazzy on-board diversions scheduled throughout each day and evening. You could gamble to your heart's content in the ship's casino, play bingo, take golf lessons, or attend a lecture on "Secrets to a Flat Stomach." (My advice for maintaining a flat stomach would have been to leave the ship immediately.) If you felt just plain lazy and had a few extra bucks, you could have forked over $125 and gotten an hour-long peppermint and seaweed massage. (No, I didn't make that up).

At the ship's swimming pool I was a spectator at a hairy-chest contest where a dozen or so male passengers willingly stripped to the waist to exhibit their manliness. A woman who was vigorously lapping up liquid refreshment at the poolside bar was selected to be the contest judge. The lady judge immediately leaped from the barstool and began her assignment. She took a very personal interest in each contestant, closely inspecting his chest hair (I'll avoid further details). Needless to say, I wasn't a participant. However, with my bypass-operation scars, if they'd held a "scary chest" contest, I would have been a real contender.

On the first day out I checked out the ship's library to get a book to read during the cruise. There wasn't much of a selection. Cruise ships don't encourage reading because reading interferes with organized pastimes like bingo, hairy-chest contests, and seaweed massages. (Fact: they keep the books locked up most of the time.)

Our ship docked at two ports on Mexico's Yucatan Peninsula: Calica and Cozumel. There were plenty of on-shore activities, and the local citizens have some rather unique ideas about what will amuse the ship's passengers.

Scuba diving is available where you can cozy up to tropical fish the size of Buicks but with more teeth. You could tour nearby Jaguar Island. (Note: the inhabitants of this island are *NOT* people.)

Or perhaps your preference would be a jeep ride into the Yucatan jungle to peer into giant sinkholes. For $85 you could don a space-age helmet and take a stroll on the ocean floor under twenty feet of water. The brochure stated that knowing how to swim wasn't a prerequisite. Just walk on the bottom and breathe the helmet's continuous air supply. Ah-huh. I'm not much into hair-raising pastimes anymore. The only hazardous things I did on shore were to drink the Mexican coffee and go shopping with the three women.

As usual, the food on board ship was excellent, skillfully served by a first-rate dining-room staff. Our head waiter was Boris, a Bela Lugosi look-alike with prominent eyebrows, a piercing stare, and a heavy Slavic accent. Come to think of it, I never saw Boris during the daylight hours. Seriously, Boris was an excellent waiter and insisted on attending to every last detail during the dinner service. On the first night out when I attempted to refill my own wine glass, Boris appeared out of thin air and wrestled the wine bottle from my hand.

"Vat are you doink?" he hissed in my ear. "Pouring the vine iss my chob!"

Night after night Boris served up what seemed like seventeen-course dinners. Each place setting had more silverware than I have in my entire kitchen. The appetizers were cunningly arranged on the plate to look like Salvador

Dali paintings. Entrees had unpronounceable European names. Most of the time I didn't know what I was eating, but it all tasted terrific and I wolfed it down.

All too soon the cruise was over. On New Year's Eve I waddled off the airplane in Upper Michigan, about a thousand pounds heavier than when I left before Christmas. As I searched the airport parking lot for my snow-covered car, my lungs recoiled from the frigid air. The Caribbean climate had thinned my blood.

At least something about me was thin.

A TRIP TO MUSIC CITY

Karen's children, two daughters and a son, all live in Nashville, and in June, 2009 she decided it was time for a visit. Since I'm an incurable tripaholic, I elected to tag along.

Being the capital of Tennessee is only a sideline for Nashville; most people refer to it as "Music City" or more informally, "Twang Town." Nashville has long been the home of country music.

The city's reputation for country music got kick-started in 1925 with radio broadcasts of the *WSM Barn Dance* from downtown Nashville. Shortly afterward the program was renamed *The Grand Ole Opry* and is now the oldest continuously running radio program in the United States. Some of the bands featured during the *Opry's* early days were real pickin' and grinnin' groups like the Possum Hunters, the Dixie Clodhoppers, the Gully Jumpers, and the Fruit Jar Drinkers. Top-chart country music greats that later performed on the program included Lefty Frizzell, Roy Acuff, Webb

Pierce, and Hank Williams Sr. On October 2, 1954, a teenage Elvis Presley made his first (and only) performance there. The audience's reaction to Presley's brand of rockabilly music was shock, and after the show he was told by the *Opry* manager that he ought to return to Memphis and resume his truck-driving career. Elvis never came back. A few more recent stars at the *Grand Ole Opry* have been Emmylou Harris, Loretta Lynn, Garth Brooks, and, of course, Dolly Parton.

Although Nashville is most famous for country music, this is not its biggest industry. The city is the largest publishing and book distribution center in the Southeastern United States. Also, 350 health care institutions have operations in Nashville. And they have a very strong tourist industry. In spite of the ever-present crowds that regularly converge on the city, Nashville is impeccably clean. No trash or garbage litter the landscape.

Another "notable" industry in Nashville's history dates back to the Civil War. Northern forces had taken over the city, and with its central location, Nashville became a training center for Union troops going into battle. With such a large contingent of young men in the city, prostitutes followed, and soon there was a problem. Army officials became alarmed at the rapid rise of venereal disease, and they put the women on a steamboat and shipped them up to Louisville, KY. But guess what, Louisville wasn't having any of it, and the lovely ladies returned on the same boat. In desperation the Union army elected to issue each prostitute a license, and made weekly physical exams mandatory. Nashville, therefore, became the first U.S. City to legalize prostitution. Don't pack your bags, you guys, it isn't like that today.

Karen and I stayed at the Hermitage Hotel, an elegant old establishment. When the Hermitage (named after Andrew Jackson's Hermitage estate outside of Nashville) opened its doors in 1910, they advertised the rooms as *"fireproof, noise proof, and dust proof. $2 and up."*

The guest book reads like a *Who's Who in American History.* Six presidents have made their way to the Hermitage Hotel along with such celebrities as Bette Davis, Greta Garbo, and Al Capone. Pool legend, Minnesota Fats, lived there for seven years.

In 1941 Gene Autry was a guest at the Hermitage. Just as famous, his horse, Champion, also stayed in the hotel and was cared for by the hotel staff. The horse stayed on the 4th floor and used the freight elevator to get in and out of the hotel. I wish I'd known that before we arrived, because I could have requested the same 4th floor room. For me it would have been like sleeping in the Lincoln Bedroom in the White House.

Many refer to Nashville–somewhat tongue in cheek–as the city of hope. Uncountable numbers of aspiring musicians flock to Nashville, hoping to find fame and fortune in the music business. And since the likelihood of this happening is not great, these same people must take other jobs to make ends meet. Karen and I got into a conversation with Brad Naylor, the Hermitage doorman. Naylor arrived in Nashville years ago with his set of drums, hoping to hook up with a hot band and make it big. Luckily he found a good day job at the Hermitage. Yet Naylor has made it bigger than most. His schedule at the hotel is flexible enough to allow him to travel with his band, Kink Ador, on gigs around the east-central U. S. And there's always hope (there's that word again) that someday he can give up his day job.

Everyone's heard about Southern hospitality, right? Nashville has it in abundance. The first morning I went up to the Hermitage front desk and asked for a Nashville newspaper. I had already received my requested *USA Today* in a bag attached to the outer doorknob of the room, but I wanted a local paper with the weather forecast.

The desk clerk looked embarrassed. It seemed that they only received enough morning Nashville newspapers to deliver to the doors of the guests that requested them. He searched around for an extra newspaper with no luck. Moments later another staff member joined the hunt. Very shortly the hotel manager came up and asked what the problem was.

"You can't find a newspaper for this gentleman?"

The two staff members shook their heads.

I was beginning to feel guilty about causing all the commotion. "Look, I spotted a Walgreens in the next block. I'll just go over there and get one."

The manager was having none of that. "We'll have a newspaper at your door in ten minutes."

And that's exactly what happened. I opened the room

door, and the hotel manager–dark blue suit and tie–handed me a Nashville newspaper and promised that there would be a local paper on the doorknob every morning of my stay. Just an example of Southern hospitality.

And that's what Karen and I experienced all over Nashville. Hotel staff, restaurant servers, and people on the street were more than gracious. And, of course, Karen's children gave us a very large dose of Southern hospitality by chauffeuring us around the city and showing us the sights. We loved the trip.

The one thing that Nashville could improve upon is their summer weather. It was hot. But I could easily go back for another visit . . . like in January.

WASHINGTON, D. C.– AN "AMERICAN PARIS"

I n 2009 with all the problems the government was wrestling with, I thought it was about time I went to Washington, D. C. to give newly elected President Obama the benefit of my thinking on several thorny issues. Karen said that a trip to Washington sounded just fine, but she was sure that the President wouldn't be able to squeeze me into his busy schedule. However, she said, let's go to Washington and do some sightseeing. We packed our suitcases and took off.

Heading anywhere south from the U. P. in mid-April is an excellent way to find better weather, and that was certainly true for Washington D. C. Every day we spent there was sunny with temperatures topping out in the seventies. My early-morning walks were great. Our hotel was very close to the National Mall, the mile-long grassy strip of land between the Washington Monument and the Capitol Building. At 7AM I'd go there in a light jacket and do my two miles, enjoying the early morning sun reflecting off the Washington

Monument, transforming it into a giant dazzling spire rising from the ground.

Washington, D. C. has the reputation of being home to pork-barrel politicians, conniving lawyers, and oily lobbyists. There's some truth to that, of course, but let me present a different perspective. Washington is a very interesting, uniquely beautiful city.

By U. S. metropolitan standards, it's not huge. The 61-square-mile piece of land is home to less than 600,000 residents. But at the start of a normal workday, government commuters from surrounding suburbs in Virginia and Maryland rush in, pumping the population up to over a million in a matter of hours. But at 4PM they all rush out again. In fact, on weekends D. C. is a rather serene place; the traffic is light, and there's plenty of parking spaces.

The federal government accounts for 27% of the jobs in Washington, tending to immunize the district to national economic downturns. The government and associated private companies continue operations even during recessions. As of November, 2008, the Washington Metropolitan Area had an unemployment rate of 4.4%; the lowest rate among the 49 largest metro areas in the nation. If you want job security, go to Washington.

And many of those jobs must be good-paying. As of 2011, D. C. residents have a personal income per capita of over $84,000, higher than any of the 50 states.

Washington is a city designed by a Frenchman. In 1791, President George Washington commissioned Charles

L'Enfant, a French-born architect, engineer, and city planner to plan the layout of the new capital city. L'Enfant's plan was modeled in what is called a baroque style, incorporating broad avenues radiating out from rectangles and circles, providing open spaces of landscaped green areas. Practically every block has its flower beds. Spring flowers were in bloom along with multitudes of flowering trees. We saw millions of red and yellow tulips around the city.

And the place is *CLEAN!* No graffiti on walls or sidewalks. It was rare to see even so much as a scrap of paper on the streets.

There are times–not often enough–when Congress actually does something right. In 1899 they passed a law declaring that no Washington, D. C. building could be taller than the Capitol building. Today the D. C. skyline remains low, in keeping with Thomas Jefferson's wishes to make Washington an "American Paris" with low buildings on light and airy streets.

We toured past the Capitol, the White House, the Lincoln Memorial, and the Washington Monument. We went up to the Georgetown district to see where the *REALLY, REALLY* rich and influential people in D. C. live. If you want a decent Georgetown condo, it runs about $2-3 million.

But what we enjoyed most were the art galleries and museums. We spent quite a bit of time in the National Gallery of Art, admiring up close the works of Rembrandt, Da Vinci, Matisse, Van Gogh, and many other classical painters.

Anyone who travels to Washington shouldn't miss the

Smithsonian Institution's National Air and Space Museum. Picture this: *The Spirit of St. Louis*, the airplane that Charles Lindberg flew across the Atlantic, is hanging from the ceiling just inside the entrance. Standing in their launch positions are various missiles from early U. S. space programs. But the highlight for me was getting up close to *The Wright Flyer*, the airplane that the Wright brothers successfully flew at Kill Devil Hills, North Carolina in 1903. No, it's not a replica, it's the real deal.

What was wrong with our Washington trip? Time; we didn't have enough of it. We barely scratched the surface of the Smithsonian and didn't have enough time to get down to Mount Vernon. Karen and I are already planning our next D. C. trip. Unfortunately we didn't time it right to catch the white blossoms on Washington's famous cherry trees. The day after we got home, though, our trees had white stuff on them, but it wasn't cherry blossoms.

QUARANTINED

I hadn't been to Hawaii since 1960, and I was curious to see how it had changed, so in October, 2007 Karen and I flew to Los Angeles, boarded a cruise ship and sailed to the islands. The Diamond Princess is my kind of ship, large enough that you can dine in a different ship's restaurant every night of the week. They even stocked my favorite wine, although a bottle cost me three times what I pay for it at Elaine's Place in Ishpeming. Of course, the ship's atmosphere was more luxurious than Elaine's.

I had heard that Hawaiians are a friendly lot. They give you a broad smile and say, "Aloha, piki molu wikiwiki hokai lulu," which translated means, "We extend a warm Hawaiian welcome to your tourist dollars."

Okay, so I made that up, but the Hawaiian economy does rely on tourists. And there's a lot of them there. On any given day the island of Maui alone has over 35,000 visitors which is about the same number of bikini-babes on Wakiki Beach.

But the crux of this story is the fact that my visit to the

islands almost didn't happen.

Maybe you've seen news flashes where hundreds of cruise-ship passengers and crew suddenly come down with the highly contagious Norwalk Virus.

Well, guess what happened to me.

One morning a few days out of Los Angeles, before the ship reached Hawaii, my breakfast didn't seem to be agreeing with me. Karen and I were shopping in the ship's boutiques when I had a sudden and urgent call of nature. I rushed–almost unsuccessfully–to find the nearest men's room.

I decided that it might be wise to get checked out in the ship's medical facility. I went in, filled out a form describing my problem, and turned it in to the nurse.

A doctor came out to the waiting room and scanned my form. He looked at me with alarm. "Diarrhea? You've got diarrhea? You can't sit here in public! Get to your stateroom immediately! I'll be right up to see you!"

A woman passenger sitting in the medical-facility waiting room cringed away from me as I headed out the door.

I hurried up to the stateroom, and moments later there was a knock on the door. The doctor entered. This was by far the quickest service I'd ever gotten from any physician in my entire life.

The doctor had me lay on the bed while he probed my stomach, took my blood pressure, and asked me a battery of questions.

"Is it the Norwalk Virus?" I asked.

"Yes, it is. Did you use any public toilets this morning?"

"Yes, on Deck 7"

"Which one?"

I wasn't familiar with the layout of the ship at that time. "I don't remember where on Deck 7 it was."

"Well, we'll close all of the men's rooms on Deck 7 just to be on the safe side." The doctor was driving home the fact that I'd suddenly become a threat to mankind. He went on to tell me that under no circumstances was I to leave the stateroom. I was to have all of my meals brought to me, bland food only, and drink nothing but water, plenty of water.

With the exception of quick trips to the bathroom, I laid on the bed and watched TV, half expecting to see the Diamond Princess on a CNN news flash with the caption, *Michigan Man Triggers Norwalk Outbreak on Cruise Ship.* I was now certain that all I'd see of Hawaii would be from the stateroom window.

The stateroom was off limits to the regular steward, but two men in surgical masks and rubber gloves came in twice and disinfected all of the horizontal surfaces, including the telephone and TV remote. From time to time someone in the medical facility would call, asking how I was doing, but probably also checking to see that I was still in the stateroom. Karen was bringing in bland food, carefully pushing the tray toward me at arm's length.

Late in the day the diarrhea had begun to ease, and I was actually feeling better. A nurse came by, checked me over, and gave me some medication, explaining that if no more diarrhea occurred in the next 24 hours then I could leave the stateroom and resume my normal activities and diet. I quietly laid down on the bed, scrunching up every muscle in my body, silently praying for no further explosions in my lower region.

Late the following afternoon, after 30 hours of quarantine, I burst forth from the stateroom, a well man, wanting to shout, "Free at last! Free at last!" The ship didn't experience a major Norwalk outbreak, mainly, I suppose, because the medical staff nailed me early.

So Karen and I got to see the wonders of Hawaii first hand: an awesome helicopter ride over the islands of Maui and Molokai, an actual submarine ride at Kona to view exotic tropical fish, a journey to Wiamea Canyon–a miniature version of the Grand Canyon. Even more exciting was the fact that at one port the Hawaiians provided a free shuttle from the ship to the nearest Wal-Mart. I won't mention any names, but someone I know very well took that tour.

SAN FRANCISCO

I n January, 2009 Karen and I felt that some relief from the Upper Michigan bone-chilling, sub-zero weather was needed, so we took a trip to San Francisco. Upon arriving we discovered that people in San Francisco were of the same mind, thinking seriously of flying to Hawaii to escape their bone-chilling 50-degree winter weather on the bay. Cold weather is all relative. When we got off the plane in San Francisco their 50-degree temperature felt to us like we *WERE* in Hawaii.

I didn't know it at the time, but the San Francisco hotel that we booked into has a long and colorful history. In the spring of 1906 the Fairmont Hotel was getting ready for its grand opening. But at 5:12AM on April 18th the city was jolted awake by a giant 8.2 earthquake. When the severe shaking stopped, the Fairmont was one of the few buildings in the neighborhood still standing. After repairs the hotel opened the following year and has been in business ever since.

The Fairmont is elegant. Huge marble columns grace both the exterior and interior of the building, adding stately beauty and structural support to the roof and ceilings. The columns probably saved the hotel during the big quake. The public areas have gilded mirrors, massive ornate chandeliers and intricate scroll work decorating the high domed ceilings. The hotel's location is prime, at the very apex of San Francisco's Nob Hill, providing excellent city views from every room. Nob Hill is so steep that if you stumbled and fell at the Fairmont entrance you'd roll for blocks. Hardly a place for a morning stroll.

Beginning with Teddy Roosevelt, the Fairmont has provided beds for every president of the United States (maybe President Obama hasn't made it there yet, I don't know). Celebrities including notables like Rudolph Valentino, General Omar Bradley, Chief Justice Earl Warren, Marlene Dietrich, and Clint Eastwood have stayed there. Orson Welles once got into a heated discussion in a Fairmont elevator with newspaper magnate William Randolph Hearst when Hearst objected to Welles' characterization of him in the movie "Citizen Kane." Afterward, Welles offered to buy Hearst a drink, but the offer was refused.

At the end of World War II the Fairmont hosted the International Conference which led to the birth of the United Nations. Hotel guests as well as locals dined and danced in the Fairmont's Venetian Room while they enjoyed big-name entertainment like Ella Fitzgerald, Nat King Cole, Vic Damone, and James Brown. Tony Bennett first sang "I Left

My Heart in San Francisco" at the Fairmont.

Chinatown was at the top of our list of places to visit, and we got lucky, arriving at the beginning of the Chinese Lunar New Year celebration. The Chinatown streets were packed with people enjoying the parades featuring children in costumes–many of them on stilts. The San Francisco police blocked vehicle traffic, allowing open-air food vendors to set up shop in the middle of the streets.

This was the beginning of the Chinese Year of the Ox. People born during the Year of the Ox are said to have determination and the ability to work steadily without complaint. Interestingly, President Obama is an Ox, and oh boy, does he need those personality traits!

During the Chinese New Year celebration retail merchants slash their prices to bring themselves good luck in the new year. I mean, they really cut prices to the bone. Karen and I shop for wall art whenever we travel, and we found a couple of really good buys in Chinatown.

And we did all of the other San Francisco tourist things, too. We took a double-decker bus tour through Fisherman's Wharf, Golden Gate Park, Twin Peaks, and, of course, the Golden Gate Bridge.

We hopped on a cable car and were shocked to find that a one-way fare is now five dollars. When I first visited San Francisco in 1960 you could ride a cable car for twenty-five cents.

We visited the Haight Ashbury district, birthplace of the "hippie" movement in the '60's. Gentrification has invaded the "Haight" these days with upscale restaurants and clothing boutiques, but there are still plenty of hippie wannabes wandering the streets using a lot of four-letter words as hippies are supposed to do.

We looked in the store windows in the Castro district, home of one of the largest gay communities in the world. I never realized that men's underwear came in so many different styles and colors.

And, of course, we ate. And we ate some more. There are more restaurants per capita in San Francisco than any other city in the United States, and we visited them all, enjoying great food three times a day.

Upon returning home and getting on the scale it was time to get back to veggie subs, yogurt and skim milk.

BELLAGIO:
A DIFFERENT LOOK IN LAS VEGAS

Karen and I love to go to Las Vegas. One of the things we enjoy out there is shopping for wall art at the galleries. What? You don't believe it? It's true. You see, we don't gamble. What? You don't believe that either? Sorry, but that's also true.

Las Vegas is a city of big hotels, and we spoil ourselves by staying at one of the biggest and most grand: the Bellagio. Bellagio employs over 9300 staff, enough jobs for every person in Ishpeming plus all of their Negaunee relatives.

But one of the real fascinations with Bellagio is not what it is but what it isn't. Every big Las Vegas hotel has its name plastered on the wall facing the street in four-story-high letters, accented with in-your-face flashing lights, enticing you to enter. You know what you'll find inside.

Gambling.

But that's what Las Vegas is all about, isn't it? People go there to roll dice, pull levers, and play cards, and with any luck go home with a bit more than the clothes on their backs.

Bellagio isn't like that. The entire street in front of Bellagio is a tree-lined boulevard, concealing a large part of the hotel building including its name–absolute heresy in Las Vegas.

Beyond the trees at the front of the property is an eight-acre lake. In the lake are more than a thousand fountains that regularly perform synchronized water ballet with water soaring as high as 460 feet into the air. These performances are enhanced by music and lights. (Are we really in Las Vegas or did the pilot make a wrong turn and put us down in Rome?)

The entrance to Bellagio is at the end of a long curving cobblestone driveway. Uniformed greeters rush out to open your vehicle doors, handle your luggage and direct you into the front lobby.

And you've never seen a hotel lobby like this one. The 18-foot ceiling is filled with richly vibrant, enormous floral blossoms crafted by world-famous glass sculptor Dale Chihuly. The front desk–30 yards long–is bordered by lush gardens filled with trees, plants, flowers and fountains.

The entire establishment expresses a natural green theme. Across the lobby from the front desk are the Conservatory & Botanical Gardens with flowing carpets of brilliant flowers, fountains and vines coiling up into huge trees. The trees–not real but looking real–have large friendly faces with moving eyes. The rest of the vegetation, including fruits and vegetables, is real. One of the current attractions in their massive fall display is a 2000 lb. pumpkin. The Conservatory & Botanical Gardens undergo a complete redo four times a year.

The Bellagio has other first-class attractions. The Gallery of Fine Art is committed to continually presenting intimate exhibitions featuring works by the world's most famous artists.

Escape into another worldly plane of dance, music and acrobatics with "O" by *Cirque du Soleil* theater in the Parisian-style opera house.

Like to shop? Bring plenty of money because Bellagio has a host of upscale boutiques and shops including names like Prada, Tiffany, Yves Saint Laurent, Gucci, and Dior. Fine jewelry, watches, designer shoes, works of art, elegant evening fashions and fine sportswear are all available.

Twelve restaurants provide any type of food you crave. One evening we dined at the Picasso Restaurant. A dozen genuine Picasso paintings adorn the walls. The food was excellent although the portions were a bit skimpy. The Picasso management assumes that their diners–"the beautiful people"–don't require much food to remain beautiful.

In short, Bellagio provides a special place of beauty and comfort–gardens, flowers, art, fashion and fine dining. A world that everyone wishes for, as it might be if everything was perfect. And it works. Bellagio currently enjoys a reputation of being the finest resort hotel in Las Vegas.

Do they have a casino? Of course they do, and it's not

hard to find. And even at Bellagio you'll always know you're in Las Vegas when the maid comes to your room at 11PM (this actually happened to me) to turn down your bed and is surprised to find that you're already in it.

Biography

Jerry Harju is an author and book publisher living in Marquette, Michigan. He received a degree in applied mechanics engineering from the University of Michigan in 1957 and completed his formal education with an MS in system engineering from the University of Southern California in 1985. After many years as a scientific systems manager in the aerospace industry in Southern California, Jerry began writing as a second career and moved back to Michigan's Upper Peninsula in 1996. He has now written eleven books, put out a CD set and also publishes works of other authors.